WHEN WILL I SLEEP THROUGH THE NIGHT?
AN A-Z OF BABYHOOD

WHEN WILL I SLEEP THROUGH THE NIGHT?
AN A–Z OF BABYHOOD

ELEANOR BIRNE

P

PROFILE BOOKS

First published in Great Britain in 2011 by
Profile Books Ltd
3a Exmouth House
Pine Street
London EC1R 0JH
www.profilebooks.com

A CIP catalogue record for this book is available from the British Library.

ISBN 978 1 84668 486 9
eISBN 978 1 84765 744 2

Text design by Sue Lamble *sue@lambledesign.demon.co.uk*
Typeset in Iowan by MacGuru Ltd *info@macguru.org.uk*

Printed and bound in Britain by
Clays, Bungay, Suffolk

The paper this book is printed on is certified by the © 1996 Forest
Stewardship Council A.C. (FSC). It is ancient-forest friendly. The printer
holds FSC chain of custody SGS-COC-2061

Contents

Something on the shape of this

The obvious way to write about the first year with a baby would be chronologically, month by month. But that would be to pretend that there was a neat transition from one step to another. There is nothing smooth or ordered about the first year. The first year is all over the place. It goes like this: one step forwards; nine steps back.

It goes like this when it comes to sleep. N started sleeping through the night when he was three-and-a-bit months old. He started to sleep until five and then five-thirty and then suddenly it was six. Six was definitely morning. Other mothers were envious when it happened. I didn't tell many people because I didn't want it to seem as though I was gloating. Inside, though, I was throwing a party and inviting all my friends round to celebrate. I thought sleepless nights were a thing of the past. I congratulated myself. I congratulated N on his brilliance, many times. Night after night went by and N slept quietly in his cot from seven until seven, and sometimes a bit beyond. I started to relax into it, this sleeping thing. I even started to resist the urge to jump out of bed every few hours to check that he was still breathing while he was doing his serious sleeping. Some nights I only checked on him once.

Then, at six months, he woke up again. I didn't know why he was awake, but he unquestionably was. I pushed the large toy box away from the radiator in his bedroom; I thought perhaps it was stopping the room from getting warm enough. I set up the travel cot in our room and put him to sleep there, thinking maybe loneliness was making him cry in the night. I tried dressing him in more layers. I tried giving him more milk, and then less milk. I was trying to solve him as though he were some sort of puzzle I couldn't get right. I tried not to be cross with him because he was a baby and babies are allowed to wake up at night – that is what they do. I didn't know why he was awake, but I knew the best way to calm him down, and so I cuddled him back to sleep at two, three or four in the morning, against all the advice of the baby books. (The baby books. I will come back to those.) After a few months of night-wakings, he started to sleep through again. The difference was that I didn't take the sleeping for granted any more. Which is just as well. He is a year old now, and he is waking up again.

There isn't an 'it's all over with' moment in the first year, and there doesn't seem to be an 'oh, so now he/she does that' moment either. N rolled onto his side when he was four months old. I thought, wow, he's on his side, and I called D to come and look and D ran downstairs and the two of us stood over N as he lay on his side on the mat. 'Wow,' said D. He was impressed. We stood there staring at N lying on his side. After a while, he rolled onto his back. We stood and watched and waited for him to roll onto his side again. He stared up at us staring down at him. He stayed where he was, flat on his back, and then we gave up watching. As it turned out, he didn't roll onto his side again for many months. He had rolled once, he knew he could do it, and he didn't want to do it again. He had a similar attitude to feeding himself. At six months, he fed himself a baby rice cake. He held it in his hand and put it in his mouth and chewed it. I was very, very excited about this. He ate nearly half a rice cake all by himself. The next day I got out the rice cakes and put one on the table in front of him. He picked it up and threw it onto the floor. I picked it up and gave it back to him. He threw it onto the floor again. I picked it up again. And so it went on. At twelve months, he hasn't fed himself a rice cake since. He likes me to break the rice cakes into tiny bits and feed them to him one crumb at a time. Sometimes I pop the bits into his mouth, sometimes I let him take them off the palm of my hand, the way you might feed sugar lumps to a pony.

The way you feel doesn't get progressively anything during the first year. You don't get progressively less or more tired. I didn't get much sleep in the first three months, for obvious reasons: newborn babies need to feed every three hours or more and feeding takes them a long time. I got a bit more sleep in the three months that followed. But at exactly six months, for whatever reason, I hit a breeze-block wall of tiredness. It wasn't only the fault of N's new night-wakings.

I was sleeping much more than I had in the early days, but sometimes I could hardly move. I just wanted to lie down wherever I happened to be – in the park, in the supermarket – and fall asleep. I wasn't the only person to feel this way: other mothers I knew with babies the same age reported a similar thing. Women with six-month-old babies don't want to meet people for lunch or go shopping or do whatever else they have stupidly said they will do; they just really, really want to go to sleep NOW. The tiredness comes and goes. Some days it is so bad you think you can't drag yourself out of bed to go to work, that you just have to stay home and sleep. Most days, you tell yourself that it is fine, that you are fine, that you'll survive the lack of sleep, that this is what lots of people do.

Time doesn't move in a straight line in this first year. It does funny things. It goes slowly, slowly, ever so slowly in the first few weeks, and then gets faster, faster, faster still. The first three months seem like six months. I think it's because of the sleeplessness; you are awake for maybe eighteen out of every twenty-four hours, so these weeks really are longer than any other weeks you have ever lived through. But then towards the end of the first year, the weeks and months speed up and shoot by in a blur and before you know it you are telling people your nearly-one-year-old son is ten months, because you have lost track of the last two months and hardly know they have happened.

I hope I have made my point about things not progressing in an ordered fashion. To be true to the experience of the first year with a baby, I should probably take out a crayon and scrawl all over the page. It's chaos, at first. But it's hard to write total chaos and it's even harder to read it.

Trying to calm N down one evening, I find myself staring with him at the giant ABC fabric letters on his mantelpiece. These are the first things I bought for him, before he was born. N loves these letters. He likes staring at them, trying to speak the sounds. I decide I will write about this first year through the shape of the alphabet – a thing that is arbitrary, basic and childish. I will write as many – or as few – entries for each of the letters as I need to. So what follows here is an A–Z. I am not claiming in these entries to be representative of anyone other than myself, and I am not claiming to have found the experience especially easy or especially hard. This is just how it happened to me. This account repeats itself from time to time, but there is a lot of repetition when looking after a baby. It is rough and raw in places, but I have felt a bit rough and raw this year too. It jumps about all over the place, but then I have been jumpy all year. I have not stayed still and nor has N.

*It should start with A, but in this case
B comes first …*

 is for before

It is the day before my due date. I am trying to let myself get bored. I need to get bored so that the baby gets bored and decides it is time to be born. I have convinced myself this is the only way it is going to happen. I am not very good at making myself do nothing. I am good at rushing off to see exhibitions and meeting people in cafés on the other side of town. But today I am going to experiment with not doing any of that. I am fed up with the phone calls from people asking if there is news. I am going underground until this baby arrives.

My doing-nothing-all-day plan has so far involved drinking a lot of tea, reading the paper, and trying to stick our wedding photos into an album. I woke up certain that if the photos didn't get stuck in today, they never would. But when I sat down to get on with it, I discovered that the album I had bought had too few pages, which means the photos will not be getting stuck into anything today. Perhaps they never will.

I am annoyed about the photo album, but – bizarrely, mercifully – I am no longer anxious about the fact that I am shortly going to have to go through labour. I have always been terrified by the idea of childbirth. The fear of it has followed me around throughout this pregnancy. I am not sure what has happened to the terror exactly, but for whatever reason (strong fear-numbing-hormones, I suspect), here I am, a day before it is all supposed to kick off, quietly padding around the house, worrying about photos and wondering where the window cleaner I booked has got to. Yes, I have booked a window cleaner because we have lived in this house with its dust- and plaster-coated windows for a year and I have suddenly decided we need to get them cleaned, right now, at this very moment. I don't like housework and don't usually notice dirty windows. But the window cleaner has not turned up and this is making me more anxious than I could have thought possible. I am an about-to-go-into-labour cliché. I am on the conveyor belt of childbirth now and I can't get off.

I am impatient about everything and I want this particular thing that has been casting a shadow over the past few months of my life, like a dentist's appointment scheduled to last several days looming on the calendar, over and done with. But my baby is in no hurry to do anything at all. He spent the first eight or so months lying sideways across me, stretched out like a sunbather. Just as I was getting my hopes up about an elective Caesarean, he flipped himself lazily into the correct position. So now here we are, the two of us, waiting it out together, but I can tell he is in no rush whatsoever, while I just want to yell: 'GET A MOVE ON, CAN'T YOU?'

Every time I walk past the spare room – now a nursery – I have to look inside. I have to check that the Moses basket is still there, that the changing table and baskets full of nappies are all in order. I rifle through the chest of drawers crammed with borrowed babygros. I find this room reassuring. It is a reminder that a baby should soon be here to make use of all the equipment we have collected for him: the blue plastic bath from Ikea, the thermometer to measure room and water temperature that D set up days ago, the giant fabric alphabet letters that I've lined up on the mantelpiece – A, B, C. I wonder what the baby whose room this is will be like. I think he will be gentle. I have had an easy pregnancy and he has always seemed calm to me, lying on his side for most of it, sleeping at night, not keeping me awake with somersaults like I've read he is supposed to. He saves his somersaulting for the daytime. It's exciting and still impossible to believe that he'll be here soon. I am impatient to meet him. Being pregnant is a bit like walking around with a wrapped-up box, and looking at it every day, trying to work out what it might be like inside, while being told that you cannot open it for nine whole months.

is for after

Now that we have N, I can't remember what life was like without him. I know it was less fun. I know there was less laundry and less washing up and that I fitted into much smaller clothes. But I can't remember what our weekends were like before we woke up to him calling out to us from his cot next door. I can't remember not being able to take him out in his buggy to show him the ducks. I can't remember a time before bath time, before the kitchen table was smeared with purée at every meal. He is so completely himself that I sometimes wonder where he came from. I have a kind of amnesia about him at any age other than the one he is now; it feels as though he has dropped in, complete, this curious, strong-willed, red-haired boy. As I look over at him, playing with the zip on his cloth toolbox that is filled with cloth tools, I find the idea that he used not to be here – that he wasn't here this time last year – too confusing. He is him and he is here.

 *E I O BLUE*

On our living-room wall we have a large print in a frame. It is blue with large white capital letters stencilled onto it, spelling out *A E I O BLUE*. It is very long and hangs over the sofa. Aged ten months, N loves to sit in front of it. He looks up and lifts his hand in its direction and murmurs. Then he looks at me and back at the picture again. This is my cue to spell out the letters to him, so I do, pointing at each one in turn. 'A', I point; 'E, I, O, Blue.' And he smiles. Then he lifts his hand and murmurs and looks at the picture and back at me, and this is my cue to read it again. Whenever he catches sight of the picture from down on the floor, or if I lift him up to take him to bed and he finds himself level with it, he smiles and smiles at it. Whenever he sits on the sofa with us, he cranes his head to look back and up at it hanging on the wall behind him. It is the most curious thing.

acks

You need a strong back to have a baby. Babies want to be carried all the time, and the longer you hold them the heavier they get. When N is a few months old, D's back gives way completely. He can't walk, he can't sit; he can only lie flat on his back and when he wants to move he gets on his hands and knees to crawl. Now I have two babies – a giant, crawling one, and a smaller, non-crawling one, both of whom need waiting on hand and foot. D's damaged back scares me – not because I am scared for him that it will not get better, but because I am scared for my own selfish reasons that it will not get better, because he can do nothing around the house, can do nothing at all while his back is like this. I spend my days feeding N and lifting him and changing him and shushing him, and then when he is asleep in his Moses basket I carry things about the place for D instead: trays of food and books and packets of Ibuprofen. After a little while – I forget how long – D's back gets better and he can walk again and carry things and help with N. My own back is holding out quite well so far. I have to be careful not to hold N for too long because it starts to nag and twinge if I do. I don't always hold him as long as he would like me to in the night, and then I put him down too early and it all goes wrong. Parents-to-be should be given an all-over MOT before their baby is born, with dodgy backs assessed and intensive physio given, or whatever else it takes to shore them up for the crucial carrying years ahead.

I love N's back. I love feeling the length of it under his clothes when I hold him up on my shoulder. It feels long and sleek, self-complete. When he was a newborn, his head bobbed, bob-bobbed when I held him to my shoulder. He was like a hungry kitten or a puppy. Later, he stops bobbing. At five months, he holds his head up and looks over my shoulder and sometimes gives a little sigh, as if to say, yes, finally, this is what I wanted, to be up here. And I stroke his back as he does it.

Bath time

Bath time is N's favourite part of the day. Until he was about seven months old, he used to cry to be taken up to his bath at six-thirty exactly, as if he had some internal alarm set to remind him of this event. At nine months, it happens a bit later but he still screeches for joy when I carry him upstairs to the bathroom, and kicks his legs as he lies on the bath mat, waiting for the water to (quarter-)fill the tub. He still refuses to sit up in the bath. It is his view that baths are for lying luxuriously in – and I agree with him. He stretches out to his full length, staring at the shiny silver taps. Sometimes he splashes like mad, soaking whoever is bathing him, kicking water into his own eyes. On other days, he just lies there, calm and reflective, eyes on those taps, very serious. He likes to try and catch the water we pour out of his plastic cups for him; he can't work out why it is so slippery. When it is time for him to come out of the bath, I count down from five, slowly, and he looks up at me and grins. He likes the countdown. Do numbers interest him, or is it the rhythm of it, the anticipation? Then he's up in the air, naked and wet. I dive him down onto his laid-out towel as fast as I can and fold him into it. I scoop him up and turn him to face himself in the bathroom mirror so that he can smile at himself in his hood. Then it's upstairs to get dressed to the sound of the singing Fisher Price clock, where sometimes screaming happens, followed by milk and – bliss – bed and sleep.

Before (again)

There is a door you walk through that separates the pregnant you from the mother-of-a-baby you. When you are pregnant with your first baby you aren't able to think about what is coming next. You feel superstitious about it, and it requires too big an imaginative leap. Six months before I was due, my friend J was taken into hospital just before her baby, G, was born. The baby was the wrong way up and they didn't notice until the last moment, so they took her in. They didn't want her going into labour at home, they said. Eight months and two weeks pregnant, J was far from being a mother yet. She found herself on a ward surrounded by brand-new mothers and their brand-new mewling babies. Fourteen-weeks-pregnant me went to see her there. She looked terrified, and I shared her terror. She wasn't frightened about the baby being the wrong way up, or about the Caesarean she was about to have. She was frightened of the babies lying in transparent cots all over the ward. There they were, all around, evidence of what she had in store, probably only a week away, depending on when they booked her in. The new mothers looked zonked out, lying on their beds like zombies. They were not a good advertisement for surviving labour. The babies were tiny and red and very cry-y. There was a baby car seat at the end of most beds, waiting to transport these tiny babies home. J would soon need a car seat too. She would need the babygros and the nappies and she would need to know what to do. She was a week away from all this, yet a world away too, still expecting, not yet delivered. For now, we were in the same world – I had more time to go, J's time was running out. I could see she wanted to stay in it a while longer, and, in the chaos of the postnatal ward, I didn't blame her.

I went back to visit J a few days after the birth. Now she had passed through the door and I was left trying to guess what was going on behind it, over where she was. She sat up in her hospital bed holding G in his green babygro. She was exhausted, she said everything was sore. She asked me did

I want to hold him? I said I'd never held a baby before, and she said neither had she until three days ago and I should start getting used to it. Holding G, worried I would damage him, I was dimly aware that I was holding two babies as I balanced him on my still quite small bump. I handed him back as soon as I could. J took him and fed him and looked tired and wise. She looked transported.

iology

Now that I have had a baby I no longer underestimate the importance of biology. I am now fully, properly aware that if we decide to have another baby it will be me who carries that baby and me who interrupts my life, my work, my body in order to have it. D will have to take time out too, of course; he will be exhausted and confused and all the rest of it. But I will be the one who will grow more and more lumbering and useless as the months go by. I will be the one who takes on that temporary, not-really-fully-here-now status at work that all pregnant women have because everyone knows they will be gone soon, off having a baby, off in another world completely. And after the baby is born I will be the one who will take more months out to feed and look after him or her, and who will be incapable of doing anything other than looking after that baby (as well as N) for the first few months. I will not be able to go to work and talk about normal things as though the whole world has not changed for ever, although D will be able to do this – he will be *required* to do it. It will not be business as usual for me. When I think about the next five years and the fact that at some point we will want another baby, it makes everything I am doing now feel short-lived and temporary. This is being in limbo time.

ody

In the months after giving birth, my body gives up on itself, like it has had enough. No one tells you that, between them, pregnancy and birth knacker your body out completely. I am not that interested in my own body any more. I am grateful to it that it let a baby grow inside it and then come out of it. But I feel distant from it now, almost as though I have mislaid it somewhere. My body feels like an old coat I have grown out of, an old coat that is more than a little worse for wear, but that I can't be bothered to repair.

The first signs of my body's wear and tear show themselves when N is about ten days old and my blood pressure suddenly shoots through the roof. I start seeing wavy lines where bookcases and vases of flowers should be. The community midwife tells me I might be about to have a stroke or at least an epileptic fit. When she tells me this the wavy lines start dancing and pulsing extra hard. I am sent off to casualty, where they ask me lots of questions. They want to know my baby's name and if I can see his face properly. They give me strong drugs and stick me up on a hospital ward with N. The drugs make my arms and legs swell up until they feel like balloons about to burst. They also give me heart palpitations and head rushes like I haven't had since I was a teenager. I am allowed home after a few days, after the medication has brought my blood pressure down to something resembling normal, but the head rushes and palpitations continue. For weeks I am too out of it to wonder whether it might still be the drugs that are making me feel this way. I assume it is the lack of sleep, or possibly something related to postnatal depression. The community midwives who come to check up on me are big on the idea of postnatal depression, as is the health visitor. It is something they have been told to watch out for. But then D reads the side-effects leaflets that come with the medication and tells me to go back to the doctor. I am on two different pills twice a day and I beg her to let me come off them. She agrees to let me start to cut down, slowly. Gradually, the palpitations calm down and I stop getting head rushes when I try and do anything in a hurry. Sometimes trying to fix things just makes them worse.

My body is failing me in other ways, too. When N is two months old my hands are so stiff in the middle of the night I can hardly move them. They are the useless hands of an old lady. I have to wake D to open cartons of formula for me because my thumbs won't work to do it. Sometimes, as well as the stiffness in my hands, there are pins and needles shooting up and down my arms. I look the symptoms up on the internet and read about carpal tunnel syndrome, which some pregnant women get. It is something to do with the nerves and apparently it will pass. I have issues with my legs, too. When I get out of bed in the mornings I can barely walk; my ankles feel fused to my legs. I hobble stiffly, ago-nisingly, down the stairs to the bathroom. I am bent double, huddled over like a question mark. What is happening to me? I go to the internet again and am told it's because the hormones that were relaxing my muscles while I was preg-nant are now leaving my body. I am feeling more and more decrepit as each day goes by; I feel as though I have aged forty years.

Three months after N's birth I am very, very fat. I am fatter now than I was just after giving birth. I have been eating a lot of cake because the breast-feeding – or perhaps the blood-pressure tablets – have been making me weak and dizzy. My stomach is covered in small red stretch marks. None of this matters. But the stiffness and the fatness make me feel old. I am thirty-two and I hobble about and wonder if after all this I have developed arthritis. I have grey hairs, and a few white ones too. The things no one tells you.

ooks

At nine months, N loves books, which everyone seems to find very amusing, since both his parents work with them. His favourite books are made out of cloth and rustle when he touches them. He leans back on his doughnut cushion and reads the big, red one with the butterfly on the front, like an old man reading a newspaper in his deckchair. He turns the pages intently, now and then stopping to rub a green leaf or laugh at his reflection in the mirror on the back. When he is finally finished with it, he casts it aside like someone casting aside the Sunday papers having spent hours reading them, only to pronounce that there was nothing interesting in them at all. Then he will reach for the smaller, yellow cloth book which has animal tails poking out of it and makes a jungle noise when you press the cover. He will take hold of each tail and slide his hand along it, feeling the furriness of each one in turn, and playing with the tassels at the end of the yellow one belonging to the giraffe. He has not yet worked out how to make the jungle noise himself, so I press the cover for him, and the parrots squawk and he smiles in amazement, as though he has never heard this sound before. I push the buzzer again and he smiles some more, slowly looking up and down the page, taking in the jungle scene.

He has books made out of paper and board, too. His grandmother has bought him a set of books with things to touch on every page – plasticky leather bear paws on the bear picture; spongy dinosaur spikes on the dinosaur. N resolutely refuses to touch what he is supposed to touch. He keeps his hands clamped to his sides. I rub my finger over the bear paws, I stroke the fuzzy dinosaur spikes, and he watches, leaning back on me, breathing hard through his nose in apprehension. Clearly, touching is dangerous, something only a fool would risk doing. He is happy to hit the part of the page that is picture, that does not have things stuck on it, but he will not go near the risky bits. He has some board books with bright, heavily outlined images of a mouse getting up to all sorts of things – dressing up, playing the guitar, paddling in a paddling-pool. He laughs when we get to the double page with the mouse dressed up as a pirate. He stares and stares at the picture of the mouse making a cake with butter, eggs, sugar, flour and something brown that I tell him is chocolate powder but am not really sure about. He smiles when we get to the last page of the book, where the mouse is cuddling a panda. He doesn't like it when I shut the book and put it down on the mat. He whines. I try to distract him with a maraca, shaking it in front of him, but he can't take his eyes off the cover of the closed book. He stares at it and grizzles so I pick it up and open it at the first page and start reading again.

At nearly ten months, he learns how to turn the pages of these board books himself. He picks up the edge of the page between thumb and forefinger and flips it over, fast, like a bored receptionist racing through a magazine. I hardly get the chance to finish the few words on the page before it has been grabbed and turned and we are on to the next one. He doesn't get tired of this turning. We reach the end of the book and immediately have to go back to the beginning, to race through the pages all over again.

In the evenings, before his bath, we read him Roald Dahl and he laughs and laughs at the cockney accent we give the BFG, and the crazy words Willy Wonka comes out with. He grabs at the book's pages, kicks them with his toes.

ottles

If your baby is under six months old, and you do a bit of bottle-feeding, you are made to feel like *a very bad mother*. You are made to feel this by all sorts of people. Mothers who are breast-feeding babies the same age, and mothers who breast-fed now older children are the worst. They peer at you with your bottle and tell you they breast-fed *their* babies until they were five years old or something ludicrous. They look at your baby drinking happily from his bottle and pity him. Every time you get out the bottle, you find yourself making excuses.

Bottle-feeding is actually a euphemism for formula feeding; bottle-feeding a baby expressed breast milk (which I also do a lot of) seems to be acceptable in the eyes of other mothers. There are, I discover, some good things about bottle-feeding. For one thing, anyone can do it, including the baby's father, which is useful, because with a newborn, more than the endless changing and burping and carrying, it is the feeding that takes up most of the time. In the early months, when I am made to feel like a leper for using some formula (even though I am using it on the advice of the hospital), I read everything I can about the issue of formula v. breast-feeding. I take great comfort from articles suggesting that the NHS is overpromoting the advantages of breast-feeding. I nearly feel vindicated when I read somewhere that the claims that breast-feeding results in a higher IQ/stronger immunity/ fewer allergies have been wildly overstated. I quote these articles back to breast-feeding mothers like some lunatic. I clearly have a lot more guilt about this formula enterprise than I will allow myself to admit.

I do a mixture of breast-feeding and bottle-feeding for about three months (a regime started by the midwives at the hospital, with whom I have growing problems). Around this time, N decides he prefers the bottle and screams when I try to put him to my breast. I can't help but take the screaming personally. I persist for a bit, but so does his screaming. In the end I give in and stick to giving him bottles, first with expressed milk, and then when that starts to run out, with formula. Feeds now take just half an hour rather than three times that long. Both of us feel liberated. I now have two and a half hours between feeds, and N can spend more of his time lying on his back, smiling at the clouds overhead and kicking his legs.

Brighton

When N is two months old, my oldest friend, K, has a hen party. I am going to be her bridesmaid in a few weeks, complete with my not-yet-deflated stomach (the horror!). But first I have to go to the hen do.

I have been preparing, military style, for my departure, and the fridge door is crammed with bottles and bottles of expressed milk, as well as back-up formula cartons. There is enough milk to last N all week, though I am only going for the day. I have packed my breast pump in my bag, along with the pink feather boa I am taking along for K. I walk to the local market with D, pushing N in the buggy. I am going to walk on on my own from here and catch a bus further down the road. I am filled with a sense of dread. I am going to have to get on a train and go to Brighton; I am going to be at least two and a half hours away from N if he needs me. I am scared of being on the train on my own and scared of leaving him. I have not done anything – not even brushed my hair or eaten a slice of toast – on my own since N arrived. Now I am going to have to travel to another city. When I was a teenager, I went through a phase of not being able to go anywhere without company. It was a kind of agoraphobia. I worry it might be back.

Somehow, I manage to leave D and N at the market. I walk away and I can't look round because if I do I will go back to them. I am crying as though I am not going to be seeing N for a month, when in fact I am going to be back home with him tonight. But it is only ten a.m. and there is a whole day to go before then; the evening is hours and hours away. When I get on the bus there is a woman with her baby in a buggy and I want to shout: 'I have a baby too.' I feel completely lost, sitting here without N. He has only been here for a few weeks and already I have forgotten how to exist alone. At the station, I buy tickets and a newspaper that comes with a free giant bar of chocolate. I board the train. I sit opposite a group of excited girls who are taking photos of each other on their mobile phones. As the train moves out of London I eat square after square of chocolate. I imagine how I must look to the girls opposite: a fat, gloomy-looking woman who should be on a diet, scoffing a massive bar of chocolate. I wonder if any of them will find themselves eating chocolate and feeling sorry for themselves on a suburban train the first time they have to leave their new baby because the world calls, friendship calls.

I pull myself together when I get to Brighton. I take a taxi to the bowling alley where the other 'hens' are drinking pints of lager and wearing funny bowling shoes. I order a Diet Coke because I am breast-feeding and need to save my alcohol allowance until later. I turn on what I hope looks like a proper smile. I have told myself I must not talk too much about N. I have told myself I must try to act as though I am unchanged. Because here I am back in the world, which has been carrying on its normal business all this time. I hurl a heavy bowling ball down the alley. It misses most of the pins. As I walk up to take my second go, everyone watches me, and I feel like an actress on a stage.

Bubbles

Aged eight months, N loves bubbles more than anything: even more than books, though maybe not more than the bath. We have developed a new routine. When I get home from work, I lay him on the sofa and blow bubbles with the plastic wand, and he laughs and laughs. I blow lots and lots of bubbles and he stretches up into the air to catch them, batting at them wildly, giggling when they burst on his face.

Earlier, at five o'clock, I ran down the stairs of the office (twenty flights) and out onto the street. I ran for a bus through the rain and just caught it. I ran from the bus into the train station. I stood swaying on an overcrowded train. I walked quickly through the churchyard and down the street to our front door. And now here I am, sitting on the sofa with N, blowing bubbles and watching him laugh. This is the best part of the day. All the racing and running and panicking about missing things and here we are with these lazy, slow bubbles.

uggy

The buggy was our biggest purchase before N was born, except that we didn't buy it, my parents did. We knew which one we wanted from watching other people pushing buggies, which we did, obsessively, from the moment we found out I was pregnant. But I didn't authorise the purchase of our own model until a month before N was due; I didn't want to be overprepared. Our buggy is sleek and modern, all curves and lightness, a deliciously masculine khaki-green (we felt it was important to be camouflaged). Once we had bought all the extras – the newborn nest, the sun parasol, the ridiculous cup holder, the cocoon sleeping bag for when the baby outgrows the newborn nest, the fleece to go on the seat when it is summer and therefore both the nest and the cocoon are redundant – I calculated that the buggy plus its bits was worth more than our car (we have a very old car).

One reason we bought this buggy, other than the fact

that it looks nice, is that it is possible to have the baby facing you in its seat, in a variety of useful positions: lying down, half-sitting, properly sitting. The facing position means you can talk to your baby as you buggy along. It is supposed to help with early language development, or so the books claim. D in particular is big on the idea of early language development. The only problem, we discovered when N was about three months old, was that N didn't want to face us. He would scream as we rolled along, and raise his arms, desperate for one of us to free him, to lift him out. After a few weeks of screaming we decided to perform an experiment. We stopped on the corner of a pavement and I held N while D lifted the buggy seat off the chassis and turned it round to face the other way. I strapped N back in. He was now facing the world. We started moving. N did not scream. We trundled along and D nipped past to walk in front of him, to see what his face was up to. 'He's smiling,' he said. From that day on, we let N look at the world, not us. I tried not to think about the fact that he could be doing this in a buggy that cost half the price, and instead tried to enjoy the khaki hood, the curvy handles, the lovely way it steers down the street.

us

For his first Christmas, D and I buy N a red wooden bus with little people sitting in it. D sits with N and pushes the bus about in front of him. He makes a 'brrrrrmmmm brrrrrrrrmmmmm' bus noise. After a while, D gets up to go and do something in the kitchen. N reaches for the bus. He pushes it about a bit. '*Brrrrrrrrmmmmm,*' he goes. '*Brrrrrrrrmmmmm.*' Later, turning over the pages of one of his books, N pauses at the picture of the red bulldozer. He strokes his finger over the wheels. '*Brrrrrrrrmmmmm,*' he says, and looks up at me. For his first birthday, N's grandfather gives him a red wheely bug, which he is supposed to sit on and ride. He is too small to sit on it yet, so he just pushes it about. '*Brrrrrrrrmmmmm,*' he goes as the bug rolls along on its wheels. '*Brrrrrrrrmmmmm.*'

Brrrrrrrrmmmmms are red and they have wheels. This much N knows by the time he is one.

Caesarean

Unlike most pregnant women, who have a panic attack at the very word, I have decided I want a Caesarean. I am eight months pregnant and N is still lying sideways across me. He is having a lovely, lazy time; he is in no hurry to get his head down, bum up, into the correct position. I start to read up about Caesareans in the pregnancy books. The woman running the NCT course was very anti them. She prefaced her descriptions with phrases like, 'Let's wait until after lunch before we get to the depressing part', and 'If things go really wrong, that's when people start talking about the C word'. But I like the idea of a Caesarean. I like the idea that it is possible to know when and how it will happen, and that, while I won't be able to move my legs, there will be no pain and no panic.

The midwife at the antenatal check-up is very keen for me to get the baby to move into the right position. She tells me I need to spend as much time as possible sitting on a giant rubber ball. She tells me I should try acupuncture. I don't want to try acupuncture in case it works, and I don't do much sitting on the ball for the same reason. I start to plan for a Caesarean. A great weight of fear is lifted off my shoulders. The midwife tells me to think about ECV, a method by which they try to turn the baby by twisting it with their hands on your stomach. I don't like the idea of this at all, mainly because it sounds like it could hurt the baby. And I don't want them to turn him anyway. This baby knows he is doing me a favour by staying the wrong way up. The midwife books me in for a final scan to check he is still sideways before I tell them whether I want the ECV. I have already decided I will say no. Which means I might well find myself being booked in for a C-section this afternoon, for a date in about a month's time. I want it all to be settled and decided; I have always been good at planning.

I tell myself the scan is just a bureaucratic necessity. We go into a dark room and I hop up onto the bed. I think about the fact that, a month from now, I might be hopping up onto another bed in an operating theatre in this same building. I pull my top up and the technician puts cold gel and then the wand of the scanner on my belly. A shape flashes up on the screen. 'Cephalic,' the technician says. He puts his wand away. 'What?' I ask. I don't know what the word means. 'It means he's the right way up,' D says. 'He's put his head down.' D seems excited by this development. I think I am going to be sick. 'He can't be,' I say. I hadn't even felt him move.

We leave the room and I fall into a chair in the waiting

room. I put my head in my hands. 'I can't do it,' I say, and I really mean it. 'I can't do it the other way.' I am a bomb about to go off and there is nothing I can do about it. I am surrounded by other ticking bombs here in the waiting room and they all look calm and ready. I am shaking and trying not to cry in front of them. I don't know how I have let this happen to me – pregnancy. Until today I have been in denial about what it will lead to. But now it is official: there will be no C-section, and I am going to go into labour and it is going to be the ordeal of my life. I am not ready for it. I want to run away, but I can't run away from my own body.

alpol

You aren't allowed to give a baby Calpol (liquid paracetamol, available in corner shops everywhere) until they are two months old, so we don't. When N is getting on for three months I still do anything I can to avoid giving it to him. It is bright pink and syrupy-looking, not the sort of thing that seems good for babies. When he is four, five months even, N has to be screaming blue murder before I reluctantly take down the bottle and measure out a half-dose of the stuff. I ring D at work to say: 'He's really unhappy. Do you think I should give him Calpol? I don't want to, but ... '

As he gets older, we get bolder with the pink stuff, because it really does the trick. N stops moaning or grizzling or crying about his teeth after a spoonful. At night, he even goes back to sleep. At ten months, when his first teeth are trying to force their way through his gums, N is on the verge of being a Calpol junkie, we are so liberal in our usage of it. At this point, if N wakes unsettled in the night I do not even offer him a bottle of formula. I know he's not hungry, so it's the Calpol we go for. We produce a sachet and a spoon and as soon as he gets a glimpse of it, N is instantly calmer. He slurps the thick, gloopy medicine off the white plastic spoon, closes his eyes, and without any more fuss goes back down into his cot. He rolls onto his side for a moment and clasps his hands together on top of his chest, which is what he does when he is about to disappear into a deep sleep. I tiptoe out of the room, pull his door almost closed (I am not able to close it all the way) and climb back into bed.

haos

Some days with a baby are chaos. You wake up late because the baby was awake between one a.m. and four a.m. – you're not sure why, but he was, and so were you. You leave for work, late, and as you heave yourself out of the front door you realise what a state the hallway, the kitchen, the whole house in fact, is in. You get to work as fast as you can, and by the time you arrive you are ready for bed. Except you have eight hours in the office and then another few hours at home in the evening to go. You sit in various meetings and you are so tired your tongue is stuck to the roof of your mouth and you are having problems speaking. You drink a lot of coffee. You are monosyllabic through your lunch meeting.

By the time you get back to your desk you want to crawl into the small space underneath it. You find yourself pushing back on your chair and surveying the space. You spend the rest of the afternoon doing the most mundane bits of work available, because your brain isn't up to anything else. Then comes the journey home, when you just want magically to be there, without the effort of this in-between bit, and when you open the front door, the mess that is waiting for you is the mess that was there before you left. Downstairs, there is even more mess than you remember: mounds of unopened letters, washed-but-not-put-away laundry, not-yet-unpacked bags full of God-knows-what, read and unread books that are piled up all over your house – proof that your life is out of control. You can pretend, while the house is semi-tidy, that you are holding it all together, but when the mess is everywhere, it's obvious you aren't in charge of anything at all, you are just managing to get from day to day. When you get home and the house is like this, you want to sort it out because you imagine that might make you feel at least slightly sorted out too in some superficial way. And after you have put the baby to bed you do try, for half an hour anyway – you open some envelopes and throw things in the bin. But then you fall onto the sofa and order a takeaway because cooking or even taking something out of the freezer is beyond you tonight, and you want someone to bring you something for a change.

hecking

Babies look so small in their cots, or rather they look very flat. When they lie quiet and still and flat for so many hours at night it is as though they have gone away for a while. You spend all day with a wriggly, cooing, laughing, crying baby, and then at night he is unmoving and silent apart from the odd small cry. The contrast is alarming. At four months, N has just started to go to sleep in his own room at about seven every evening. So far, I have not found this new routine relaxing. I start to check on him about half an hour after he has first gone to bed, and I continue to check on him all evening. I put my head round his door just before dinner and then again just before I put on a film or pick up a book, and, later on, just before I get in the bath. And he lies there stretched out like a starfish, his chest rising and falling.

The checking does not stop once I go to bed. N learned to sleep through the night at three months. By the time he is six months he has been doing it half his life and I still have not got the hang of it. I wake at least twice in the night to go and see if he is still breathing. I stand in the doorway with my head cocked to one side to listen to the soft in-breath, the relief of the out-breath. I don't step into his room in case a creaking floorboard wakes him up, as sometimes it does. I stand there just outside, hovering, on tiptoe. I am a strange, eavesdropping, pyjama-clad tableau. I will stand there for as long as it takes to hear him take those sleeping breaths. And then, as though embarrassed to have caught myself at it again, I'll pretend that I need the bathroom, and that's the reason I'm out here on the landing at one a.m., and so I'll creep downstairs and go to the loo, and then I'll creep back up and climb quietly into bed, trying not to rustle the duvet too loudly in case it wakes him. In three hours' time, at four a.m., I will do this all over again. And then I will doze until I hear his first babbles in the morning, and then I will roll over in bed and leave D to get up to him, with the feeling that now I can really sleep, now that he has made it through the night. I wonder when I will start to sleep properly again, or if, as a mother now, I ever will.

hewing

Since N started to learn to eat at six months, he likes to practise chewing. He looks as if he has a strip of gum in his mouth, so pronounced is his chewing. He looks like a nonchalant teenager. He will sit on his mat while D and I are eating breakfast and watch as the toast or cereal on a spoon goes into our mouths and he will stare and then laugh. He is transfixed by our eating. And then he will chew on his imaginary gum a bit more. When we give him puréed vegetables, runny as thick cream, he chews it as though it is steak. His jaw goes up and down, round and round, a caricature of a serious eater.

hildcare

Everyone tells me it is important to get childcare sorted out early. At some nurseries, I am told, women put their names down the moment they discover they are pregnant. It is fiercely competitive, the getting-into-a-nursery game. In the month before I go on maternity leave, I phone a nursery I have been told is good. It is in our borough but nowhere near where we live. I have found the inspectors' reports online and they have only bad things to say about the nurseries closer to our house (which is probably one of the reasons we could afford the house in the first place). But this one, a couple of miles from us, sounds great, so I make an appointment to go and take a look. D and I are shown around by a friendly French woman. The nursery is white and bright inside. We watch a group of two-year-olds, with red patches painted on their noses, as they look at themselves in small mirrors. The nursery worker tells us they are just discovering that it is themselves they are looking at. She takes us into the baby room, which is less enticing. There are rows of cots lined up at one end in a sort of room within a room. It is, I suppose, a baby dormitory. The baby room is darker than the main room. There aren't many babies in it. One of them is lying on his back in a doughnut cushion. Another is lying on a nursery worker. The French woman points out the tunnels they can crawl through, the cloth toys they have to play with. She takes us back outside and across a hallway and into another room where the oldest children, aged three and four, are playing. They are about to go on an outing to the swimming pool; they are rushing around looking for bags and coats. It is all very cheerful.

D and I leave the nursery. D is very taken with it. We agree we will put the baby's name down. Later, at home, I print out the forms. CHILD'S NAME, it says at the top. Our baby is not yet born. He does not have a name. I think of the name we like best so far. Then I write it. N—, and his surname, S—. It is the first time I have written down this name that still may not become his. I sign the forms and send them back with a cheque to reserve a place. I feel pleased with myself. This is a major job done. Our childcare has been arranged. Or so I fondly think.

Christening

We decide we should get N christened because the school opposite our house is C of E and you only get to send your child there if you go to the local church. Never mind that it is fifty metres from our front door and that we hear the children in the playground there three times a day, and that the parents park their cars and stand outside our house in the mornings and afternoons when they are dropping off and collecting – N will only be allowed in if we go to church, i.e. if we agree to get God. I ask my oldest friend, K, if she will be godmother, and then we ask N and L to be godfathers. That's the easy part done. We think it would probably be diplomatic to go to a church service or two before we ask the local vicar if he'll christen N. The services are at ten a.m. on Sunday mornings.

Ten a.m. on a Sunday with a very small baby is a challenge. We make two attempts and fail; the first time I fail even to get out of bed. On the second attempt I am out of bed, but none of us is dressed or breakfasted. On the third Sunday we are determined to make it. We have been emboldened by meeting the junior vicar (I don't think this is actually his title) when we stepped into the church to look at a local planning application. This junior vicar was excited to see us. He told us about a bible-reading group that meets in the local pub on Monday nights. He thought it would be just the thing for D. He saw the leaflet on baptism I'd picked up from the table on the way in, and told us we should do it. He was, in fact, very, very keen that we should do it. So this Sunday we decide to make a concerted effort to get to the church, and we even, third time lucky, arrive on time. It is pretty full and there are lots of children. Is everyone here for the school places? The service kicks off. There is singing, which I'm fine with. Then the senior vicar gets up and starts talking about what went wrong with the mass-christening the previous Sunday. It was a disaster, he says. More than one family, he says, walked out. People were angry; it hadn't been what they were expecting. Ten babies was, on reflection, too many to baptise in one day. He says he feels he needs to apologise to those in the congregation who were victims of verbal abuse. I start to feel sorry that we missed the spectacle, and want to hear more, but then he starts talking about the coming harvest festival. N starts to get grizzly in his buggy. I start to get grizzly in my pew. I look at my watch and it says five to twelve. We have been here for two hours.

After the service, we give N his bottle in the church. There is tea and cake and chatting and D is accosted by enthusiastic members of the Monday evening bible-reading group. They smile eagerly and are excessively friendly. The junior vicar sails over, all cheery. More and more smiles. More and more enthusiasm. I can't bear it. I put N's half-drunk bottle away and drive him out. D follows behind us. He has to stop to shake hands with another man in robes when we reach the steps, but I buggy on past him. I suspect we will end up moving house before N gets to school age. I suspect this will involve us moving cities.

K – N's would-be godmother – asks me when the chris-tening is going to take place. 'We've not set a date yet,' I say, vaguely.

lapping

Aged eight months, N likes clapping. He hasn't worked out how to clap his own hands together. But if I clap my hands, he wants to hit one of my hands with his own. Or he slaps his hand on his leg, copying my rhythm. He first learned to do this in the bath. He slapped it and it made a sort of clapping-like noise that he was so pleased with, he did it for about ten minutes non-stop. When there's music on, or when he's playing with his plastic musical toy, he claps his leg to the beat.

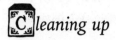leaning up

There is a lot of cleaning to do when you have a baby. There is the high chair to wipe three times a day, and the floor underneath it, also three times a day. There is the water to mop up when you have given the baby the sippy cup to hold and he has splashed it everywhere. This cleaning is all related to the top end, but of course there is the bottom end, too. The changing mat needs wiping, and sometimes the changing table it sits on, and if you are unlucky, the walls next to it, too.

lothes

The odd names given to baby clothes seem designed to indicate that you are entering a new and foreign country the moment you start shopping for them. In the weeks before N was born, my friend J, whose baby was six months old by then, sent me a list of the clothes and other bits of equipment I would need. Here are some of the items from her list. Now, many months on, I understand what they mean:

Sleepsuits

N is nearly ten months old now and I am still not sure what a sleepsuit is – another way of describing a babygro, perhaps? If that's the case, we own lots of them (giant ones now that N is older, which probably make him look like a monster baby, and which he is not allowed to wear outside the house for that very reason). If a sleepsuit is in fact something else, then N is missing out. Whatever they are, J thought we needed five newborn ones and, as she instructed, we bought a pack.

Scratch mitts
On her list, J suggested we would need scratch mitts, a term I found especially puzzling. We discovered them in John Lewis (where you can find everything). It turns out scratch mitts are tiny gloves that look like white egg-cup cosies. They are designed to stop a newborn from scratching his or her face, which is something they like to do a lot. A scratch mitt is in fact an anti-scratch mitt. We bought two sets but N hated wearing them, so we never made him.

Snowsuits
J offered to lend me one of these. I thought she was joking, since the idea of skiing, with or without a newborn, strikes me as an insane thing to do. A snowsuit, I know now, is a thick, padded, all-in-one coat with legs, like a thermal babygro with a hood. The word 'snowsuit' is unbearably cutesy. N has two, both of them lent to him. One has little bear ears on its hood and gives me a static electric shock when I touch it.

Long-sleeved body suits

J advised me to get a pack of long-sleeved body suits. I began to worry about the difference between a long-sleeved body suit and a sleepsuit, because this sort of thing was starting to feel suddenly important. I had the sinking sense that I would never really qualify to be a mother. Back in John Lewis, I discovered that a long-sleeved body suit is the same sort of arrangement as a sleepsuit, but, crucially, without the legs. On the list, which was heavily annotated, J wrote that since my baby would be a March baby, he would probably need to wear a long-sleeved body suit underneath a sleepsuit. I phoned her to query this. In the summer, she explained patiently, a short-sleeved vest would do as an undergarment, but, in her view, in March I'd do best to start off long. I had not considered the issue of layers before, or the fact that a baby might need to wear more than one type of clothing. I now know that these are questions that occupy mothers of newborns obsessively. Early on, all our fears and panics and unnamed anxieties are channelled into the vexed issue of how many layers to put on. Does he need to wear a long-sleeved or a short-sleeved vest? Does he need to wear a vest at all? Does he need a cardigan over his babygro? How about a coat? Tights?

Baby nightdress

I had been under the impression that a sleepsuit was for sleeping in, but J said for newborns, a nightdress was the thing. A baby nightdress is a long dress, designed to hang down below a baby's feet, with an elasticated hem. The idea is that it allows easy access for nappy-changing in the middle of the night. This turned out to be very important.

Grobags

A baby grobag, far from being a plastic bag filled with compost for accelerated development, is a sleeping bag with holes for the head and arms and a zip-up front. It's supposed to be a safe alternative to blankets: not even the wriggliest baby can kick one off or slither down inside it.

The new vocabulary extends beyond the clothes. I now know the meanings of words such as doidy cup, Bumbo, Baby Bjorn. They are round, cosy words. They are words designed to make the user, the parent, feel safe; to make you think that if your baby uses one of these cutely-named objects, they too will be safe.

lub

After N is born, J sends me a card in which she has written: 'Welcome to the least exclusive club in the world.' As the days and weeks go by, I realise that I really have joined a club. I like the fact it is not exclusive. Whenever I push N out in his spanking new buggy, women wheeling their babies along in the opposite direction smile at me in a knowing way. I, in turn, marvel at the ease with which these women negotiate the streets, especially when they are pushing buggies while an older child is scurrying beside them or riding along, wobbly on a bike or handling a scooter. I marvel at the ability of these people to get themselves and all their children out of the house looking normal and clean at a decent time – before lunch, even! I take to smiling at these women the moment they appear like overloaded boats on the horizon. I become someone who looks into buggies to check the age, size, hair colour of each occupant. I had never realised that the world is teeming with buggies and babies.

On the bus, women nod at N and ask: 'How old?' And I start doing it too. 'How old?' I ask, gesturing towards the beautiful blond baby dressed in his snowsuit, staring calmly out at me from under the roof of his buggy. Suddenly the city is full of mothers (and fathers) mutually admiring each other's babies. The world feels more benign.

On the rare occasions that I go out without N, dashing to the supermarket or the corner shop, I can't understand why people no longer smile at me when I catch their eye. I want to wear a sign round my neck on these brief, babyless forays, saying: 'I HAVE A NEW BABY AT HOME. PLEASE BE NICE.' I want to cry when a woman pushes in front of me in the checkout queue, until I remember that this is how people behave in real life, this is how it is all the time, unless you happen to be steering a very small baby in a buggy, when the rules are suspended for just a little while.

rying

I find it impossible not to pick up N and hold him when he is crying. When someone else is looking after him and I am in the house, I have to drop whatever it is I am supposed to be doing and go to him. It is a physical need – the need to hold him myself and comfort him. It is not that I think that I am better at it than other people; I can't stop myself from doing it. I know I am programmed to respond like this. When he cries out in the middle of the night, I find myself upright, on my feet, and heading for the bedroom door before I've had time to register the fact that I am awake, let alone out of bed. I am a puppet on strings and N is the puppeteer; he has taken over my controls. I used to wake up slowly, groggily, reluctantly. Now when I wake to his cries I find it hard to keep up with the speed at which I am moving.

As he gets older, I recognise different cries. He has a tired cry which is more like a crying moan: *I've had enough; I've had enough! Put me to bed!* He has an I've-just-been-woken-up cry, which is loud and angry and means *I'm so confused; I'm so confused! I want to still be asleep!* He takes great, big shuddery breaths between these cries, and his eyes are often red-rimmed from the cut-short sleep. He looks tiny and screwed-up; the sound is so very loud and he is so very small. And then there is the cry he makes when his teeth hurt, which is more like talking: *Aggghhhh Agggghhhh Agggghhhh.* He does it with his fingers in his mouth. It is his

way of telling me that it hurts. *Aggghhhh Agggghhhh Agggghhhh.* If you pick him up when he is crying like this, he will
often stop and blow raspberries instead, which is instantly
gratifying.

Cuddling

As a newborn, N spends hours cuddled up on my front. He
rolls himself up into a ball, with his legs under his tummy,
and falls asleep. I stay still on the sofa, on a chair outside, in
bed, wherever I am, and let him rest. Most of the photos of
N and me together in these early days are of him rolled up
hedgehog-style near my shoulder. He is so small, I can cup
almost the whole of the back of him in one hand. He is as
safe as I can make him.

As he grows older, he still likes being held close, but he
starts to pretend not to. As soon as he has the strength in
his upper arms, he pushes himself back on them, strain-
ing up like a seal, and then darts his head off one way and
then the other, focusing on something of crucial importance
over my shoulder – a lamp, the table, the rug on the floor.
The message: *I'm busy, I have important stuff to look at, there's
no time to cuddle.* But sometimes, if it's late in the day, or if
I've just got back from work, he gives himself away, exposes
himself as the little baby he still is, and puts his head down
on my collarbone and rests for a while. He becomes very still
and calm, and I wonder if he's remembering what it was like
to be just born. Then, once he's had enough, he raises his

head and darts about, busy again, busy looking, busy being in the world.

In the nights, if he wakes because of his teeth, cuddling is the only thing that will calm him. I hold him and he rests his head on my shoulder and goes very still. I fall back into the rocking motion. One side then the other, one side then the other. I hold him and I rock, rock; rock, rock. I am a boat.

D and me

Now we are three – always three. D and I do not see each other alone, unless you count the evenings at home after N has gone to bed (if, indeed, he has gone to bed, and is not up late with the famous teeth). I am not sure these evenings really count. Sometimes I worry about the fact we are not worried about not seeing each other properly. At these moments I like to blame D, but really we are both to blame. We won't spend money on a babysitter because we are spending all our available money on daytime child-care. Also, it feels like too much trouble to go out and leave N with someone else; it takes so much organising. And I have the suspicion that, even though we'd try hard not to, we'd spend at least part of the evening anticipating a call or a message asking us to come home. (The last time we left N with D's mother for the evening this is indeed what happened.)

We share a lot of the work of looking after N. When

we are home, we both wash his clothes, we both cook for him. At home, we are equal, but I am home more than D, because I have reduced my hours in the office. I work a four-day week: I get to the office at nine and leave at five. Unlike me, D does not leave work on time each day. In being late night after night, I start to suspect that D – almost certainly without realising it – places more importance on his job than mine. He denies it whenever I ask him, but I take this lateness, this not being home to share the chores, person-ally. If I wanted us to be truly equal again, I would go back to the office five days a week and I would not leave on time, but I do not want to do that.

We are parents first now; husband and wife second. N sleeps in our bed most nights. He comes in in the middle of the night, around three or four, when he wakes up scream-ing. If we leave him to scream in his cot, it goes on for hours. If we bring him in with us, he goes back to sleep straight away. I am sure N should not be sleeping with us like this, but I am not sure what else to do because D and I need to sleep too.

On the rare occasions we go out without N, we talk about him, because there is so much to talk about and there has been so little time in which to say it. Now we are three.

addy

D is better at playing with N than I am. He is better at making the brrrm, brrrm sounds that go with the red wooden bus than I am. He is better at dangling N by his ankles than I am. He is very good at bathing him. When I give N a bath it is often a quick dunk, in and out, at the end of the day. When D does it it's a whole new game. D is good at doing N's laundry but hopeless at putting the clean baby clothes away. D is scared of cutting N's nails because his fingers are so small and hard to hold still. When D feeds N his bottle he sits him in the daddy chair, with his knees up and N lying back against his legs to face him. You can't really know what the father of your child is going to be like until he is actually a father. I have been lucky with D.

ancing

When N is two-and-a-bit months old, the three of us go to my friend K's wedding. N is meant to go back to my parents' house in the evening, for the disco part, but for various reasons to do with sick relatives he ends up staying out with us. It is about ten o'clock and the music is cranked up loud. The DJ starts playing 'Family Affair', which D has always peculiarly loved, and we get up to dance. D is holding N against his shoulder and we start moving a bit on the dance floor. D is a very bad dancer and I am not much good either. The music gets even louder and I try not to worry about N's eardrums or the fact we are dancing next to the speakers. When D turns on the dance floor I lean over to check on N. The music is blaring and the disco lights are flashing and N is fast asleep. I wonder if the disco beat reminds him of my heartbeat, if the flashing lights are like traces of light he glimpsed when he was inside me. Perhaps life before birth is one long wedding reception disco. It is a scary thought – that N may have spent nine months in a place like this.

Towards the end of his first year, N starts dancing. His dancing is a rocking motion that comes over him when I sing to him or, more bizarrely, when I count. He always dances when we get to the page in his fish book that says: 'One, two, three. How many can you see?' He sits and rocks his upper body rhythmically. The dancing must be instinctive. I hope for his sake he gets better at it.

Deciding to have a baby

There was no definitive moment when I knew – *eureka* – that I wanted to have a baby. Rather, I became gradually aware that it was something I might want to do, and sooner rather than later. I felt as though there was something (or someone?) missing. I couldn't work out if this was premature; if it was just me being impatient because I am an impatient person and I like to be busy. We were busy enough, as it happened, as we had just bought a derelict house and were trying to work out how to go about doing it up. We didn't have a builder and we had no idea what it was all going to cost. Even so, I decided I had to tell D my thoughts on babies.

D and I did what we always do when we have something to discuss: we went to the pub. I drank a quick couple of glasses of wine before I dared bring up the subject. I was nervous and embarrassed; I felt like a cliché with my new-found baby hunger. When I finally told him, D said yes, a baby was a good idea. I said I was glad he agreed. We agreed on it the way you might agree to buy a certain kind of wall-paper, in a sure, why not, let's go for it sort of a way. And then we had another drink. I was relieved to have got the conversation over. One of us must have quickly changed the subject after that. We almost certainly talked about support-ing walls or dry rot for the rest of the evening.

Depression

I expected to get depressed after N was born. I read up about it to prepare myself. I was dreading the empty time that would come when D went back to work after the birth. Yet somehow it didn't happen. I did get shortness of breath and palpitations in the early weeks – now I wonder if these were anxiety attacks (I blamed them on blood pressure medica-tion at the time) – but they passed quite quickly. I got off lightly.

Dread

From the day he is born, I dread the moment I will have to leave N. As in properly leave him for a whole day on a regular basis. As in leave him to go to work. I can't imagine it being physically possible. In the maternity hospital, I hate leaving him even to go to the loo (I am afraid he will be stolen). Back home, I am with him twenty-four hours a day. He sits on me when he is awake and he lies on me when he is asleep. If he is sleeping in his Moses basket, the basket is always in the room with me. I need to keep him close. Sometimes, I look at him sleeping and think about the fact that one day I will have to walk out of the door to go to the office, leaving him with a stranger. I think about walking out of the door and I cry. I cry at the thought of it when N is one month old. I cry at the thought of it when he is two months, three months, four months, five months, six months, seven months old. I torture myself. I spend far too much time reminding myself it will have to happen and dreading it.

Dropping things

At nine months, N has discovered how to drop things. I give him a soldier of toast, as I have read you are supposed to, and he picks it up between thumb and forefinger, disdainfully, and lifts it to the edge of the table. Then he dangles it in mid-air before very deliberately opening his fingers and releasing his grip. The toast drops to the floor and lands on the oilcloth under his high chair. He looks down and studies it. After he has had a good look, I pick it up and put it back on the table. I would like him to try to eat his toast, but there is no chance of this happening. It has become part of a much more interesting scientific experiment. Only a crazy baby would eat a piece of toast when there is so much more fun to be had with it. He picks up the buttered soldier again, moves it to the edge of the table, and, with what looks like enormous satisfaction, releases his grip and drops it. He is like a JCB digger discharging his load, precisely and efficiently. Once again, he studies the floor. He is practically bent in half in his high chair, so intent is he on looking down at the bit of bread below him. I worry he is going to hit his head on the table. After a while, I pick up the toast and put it back in front of him. He picks it up and the whole process starts over again. So this is gravity, he seems to be saying. Wow.

leven months

At eleven months, N is starting to look like a little boy rather than a baby. As he gets older, I feel sad about his receding babyhood, but my consolation is that – so far – he's getting more endearing rather than less. When he sits babbling and smiling and banging a wooden spoon on a saucepan, with curly hair that now comes down over his ears, it is impossible to wish he was any age other than this one. When I look back at photos of him when he was three or four months old, he looks like a different baby. He has the same expression, but he is so small, so inert. The first year has charged by so fast that I can't believe he is nearly one. Even so, the baby N in these photos feels remote to me. N is who he is now. He is eleven months old and happy, banging a wooden spoon, possibly in need of his first haircut.

Evenings

Evenings are important for everyone's sanity. I mean evenings when your baby is asleep and you are free, for a few hours at least, to get on with other things, like watching TV or having a bath or eating calmly or drinking a glass of wine. Life with a newborn is tiring, not just because they do not sleep through the night, but because they do not sleep through the evenings either. If you are brave enough to try cooking a proper evening meal you must do so with a newborn strapped to your front and you must eat the meal with the same obstacle in the way. In the early days, dinner consists of things that are not too messy if dropped on a baby's head (no hot soup; pizza is handy). At first, there is no time off. But when he is four months old, N starts to go to bed in the evenings and we have them free for the first time since he was born.

And then, when he is nearly one, N gives up sleeping in the evenings again, which means we are back on duty. It is his teeth, I think. He falls asleep with his bedtime bottle and I put him down in his cot and close the door to his room. I creep downstairs hoping he is asleep for the night. But often he is awake an hour later, screaming for help. I race back upstairs to give him a dummy, which he flings out of the cot. So I pick him up and rock him. He falls asleep on me and I hold him for what seems like hours, and then I lay him down again as gently as I can – but however gently I do it, he wakes up when his head touches the sheet and he screams. I pick him up and rock him more and after a very long time I try to put him down and he screams again. I finally give in because he is gnawing at his hands and we have already given him his allowance of painkillers. I bring him downstairs and he watches us eat. After dinner we play with him until he's had enough of his toys and then we put him between us on the sofa while we watch TV, and after two hours of being up he is still wide awake and we wonder what to do next. Finally, we make up another bottle and feed it to him in his room and this does the trick and sends him off to sleep, but now it is ten p.m. and the evening is over and it is time for us to go to bed too. No evenings means no rest, unless you count sleeping, which I don't. I can handle the three a.m. wake-ups (just about), but for my long-term sanity, I need my evenings back.

Expression

Babies' expressions are purely one thing or another. When he sees something or someone he likes, N's face displays uncomplicated, unrestrained delight. He grins like the most beautiful simpleton. When something disagreeable happens – when I put him down to get him dressed, or lay him back in his cot in the middle of the night – his face is a picture of despair. He stares hard at me: he is shocked, accusing, incredulous. His mouth crumples, a caricature of turned-downness. His chin creases up. It wobbles. There is a silence while all this is happening – the betrayed eyes, the radically downturned mouth, the creased chin – before the screaming starts. I find this expression among his sweetest; I also find it knife-in-the-heart distressing. He looks as if the end of the world has just arrived and he has seen it. But then I wind up his singing clock or hand him his big fabric A to hold and immediately the bereft, boy mouth is transformed into a concentrating mouth or a smiling mouth, and the agony of three seconds ago is forgotten. These changing expressions are signs of the wildest, most out-of-control mood swings. Babies can't pretend and they can't act; their faces can only be totally honest.

eeding

For the first three months of his life, all N wants to do, apart from sleep, is feed. 'Is he meant to feed for this long?' I ask anyone who will listen. After I make a mess of the feeding in the early days, and N loses more weight than he should, I am given strict new instructions by the midwife: I should give him an hour on the breast and then top him up with formula afterwards. Each 'mixed feed' takes about an hour and a half. After I have fed him, I change N's nappy and, if they need changing, his clothes too. Then I might put him in his buggy, depending on the time of day – all this might take another half an hour in total. This leaves me, on average, one hour out of every three each day (or half an hour out of every two and a half at the beginning) to eat breakfast, lunch or dinner; drink something; go to the loo; have a shower; hang the washing out; go to the shops to buy dinner; cook dinner; hold N when he doesn't want to be put down but doesn't want to feed either. Life between feeds is manic, lived in crazy fast-forward, racing round the supermarket and then the park because both of us need some air. Then, back home, shovelling dirty baby clothes into the washing machine while holding N and trying to return unreturned phone calls. By contrast, life during feeds is static, paralysed, interminably slow. I spend it pinned to the sofa or, when it is sunny, flopped in a deckchair outside. I have never in my life stayed so still for so long.

eet

N's feet when he is born are almost unbearably tiny. They are half-the-length-of-my-index-finger tiny and they are perfectly complete with their five extremely small toes. I think about making prints of these tiny feet, but am scared to. I want them preserved, but I know this is what hospitals do to babies who don't survive birth. I can't bear to think about that, so I don't take my own set of prints; I let N's feet get bigger, like the rest of him, with no evidence to show how small they once were.

N is like me as a baby, but his feet are like his father's. When D is happy, he curls his toes tight against the balls of his feet. I can tell if he actually likes something I have cooked, for instance, and is not just saying it, by looking at his toes. If it's good, they curl up. He wriggles them too. When I give N his milk, his toes curl and he murmurs and grunts his happiness. He wriggles and twists his feet. It is curious that this is something you can inherit; that N has a genetic predisposition to toe-curling and foot-scrunching.

Finding out you are pregnant

I thought pregnancy was indigestion. I was getting stomach cramps. I couldn't eat much food. It was the men's final at Wimbledon, an epic, tense match – Federer v Nadal – and it went on for hours. I had to lie on the sofa. I could hardly move. The next morning I allowed myself the thought: I wonder? I didn't go and buy a test straight away. I couldn't face the suspense and the drama and then it perhaps turning out negative. So I waited. I waited until I finally knew in myself that I had to be. One morning at work I decided today was the day to buy the test. But still I didn't make it easy. I walked to a chemist in my lunch break. It was an old-fashioned one and the tests were behind the counter. I didn't want to have to ask for one, so I left empty-handed. I decided I'd go to Boots when I got home, but by the time I got there it was closed. By then I was beside myself. I had to know tonight! I went along to another chemist. Closed as well. Perhaps I was still trying to delay things. In the end I went to the supermarket behind our house, which was always going to be the easiest option, and bought the kit, stuffed it in my bag, then went home and didn't go straight up to the bathroom to use it.

I started to make dinner instead. I can't remember what kind of dinner; I know that it involved vegetables of some kind, because I left D peeling them when I finally snuck off upstairs to take the test. I did the business with the stick thing and then had to wait however long it is, perhaps two minutes, for the lines to appear or not appear. I think I brushed my teeth while I waited. I know that I didn't stand there watching to see if it would change or not. I left the stick on the side of the bath and decided not to look at it again until the time was up. I turned my back on it. I knew what the result would be, but still I couldn't cope with the in-between part, the last bit of uncertainty. And then, finally, I turned round and the lines were doing whatever it was they were supposed to be doing when the test comes up positive: disappearing or appearing, I can't remember which. I think I smiled because I was right. And then I think I cried a bit with relief because I was right.

When I went back downstairs, I said, 'So it turns out I'm pregnant', or something equally undramatic. I had to play it cool. I can't remember what D said or did, but I remember telling him straight away that I wanted us to carry on as normal: it was early days. He went back to peeling vegetables. I wanted to keep a lid on it. I wanted to get to three months. I think we had a glass of wine with dinner, in the spirit of being normal. I think we may have dared raise a toast.

First born

N is my first born. I cannot believe it will be possible to have this much love to give again for a second baby. People who know tell me that it is perfectly possible.

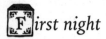irst night

N's first night with us was dream-like. For one thing, I was off my head on crazy just-given-birth hormones. The three of us had our own room in the smart new hospital. D passed out as soon as he got into bed. I think he snored. N slept too. He slept on my chest. I sat upright in bed, holding him. I stared down at him and I was in awe. I held him so carefully. I wasn't scared that he would break; I didn't feel scared at all. I just felt he needed gentleness.

Almost certainly that whole first night should have been one long nightmare, with me trying and failing to feed N and him getting cross and me getting more and more agitated at not being able to do it properly. But all N wanted to do was sleep, so I just sat there holding him, staring at him. If I could bottle any moment in my life, uncork it and relive it, it would be that night. I fell asleep just before dawn, still holding him. When I woke a few hours later, his head was next to mine on the pillow. It was indescribable finding him there like that; I recognised him straight away.

ood

At just over eight months, N isn't very interested in eating. He likes sitting in his high chair, as he is doing now, hitting the tray table in front of him. He is very interested in the picture of the yellow giraffe that sits under the clear plastic.

He likes to hit the rotating plastic toy that is stuck to the tray table with a giant blue suction pad. He likes to grab, and then throw on the floor, the bright orange lid from the top of the purée packet, and watch it as it rolls away under the dresser. But the food itself, the food that D is right now trying to spoon into his mouth, he is less interested in. He spends most of his time looking busily away in the other direction. D whistles and makes zooming sounds and, occasionally, N turns his head towards him and then D quickly takes his chance and pushes the spoon at his mouth. N takes a small sip off the spoon and then looks busily away again. He has work to do in this chair, don't we know? Eating is for wimps. Eating is for people with too much time on their hands. But the plastic lid is hilarious. Perhaps this lid here is the point of eating; the point of being strapped in a chair having a spoon thrust in your face. N takes another sip of the orange stuff, opening his mouth as wide as a tunnel and then clamping it shut again as a small mound of purée is deposited on his tongue. A twirl of the spinning plastic toy, a flick of the plastic lid, the mouth opens, the head turns, the spoon hovers and then – bingo – another partial spoon-ful goes in. It is like trying to feed an ice-hockey player while he is out there sliding his puck around. Really, N could take or leave the food, but we want him to have it; we have read in one of the scary baby books that he needs it now. The books threaten us with warnings of restricted brain devel-opment if N does not eat his orange mush at this stage. N has the orange mush smeared around his mouth, on his chin, plastered around the neck of his wipe-clean bib, and he looks like an advert for a baby in a high chair: full cheeks, food everywhere, eyes down, still concentrating hard on that orange lid. When he starts whining, D decides he is full. N turns his head vigorously away from the wipes, tries to yank his hand free from the soggy cloth, moaning about being cleaned up even at this age. And then D lifts him out of his chair, and suddenly he is free, free to have his nappy changed, free to play with his treasure basket, free for another few hours anyway, until the high chair calls again.

ridays

Once I am back at work, Friday is my day with N. Fridays make me nostalgic for maternity leave. Some Fridays we do nothing and stay in the house all day – N on his mat, me in the kitchen trying to do a bit of cooking. Some Fridays we do the opposite and do too much – music class, followed by meeting up with someone in a café, followed by a walk in the park and a visit to the swings and then the shops. I don't really mind what we do on our Fridays; I love them whatever.

riends

I have been neglecting my friends since N was born. I have shed some friends and some of them have shed me. The friends who have stayed are, on the whole, the ones who are most interested in N. I feel no one can be truly interested in me if they are not interested in him, too. The friends I have kept are, on the whole, the ones who have at some point made the effort to travel from their part of town to see us here. They are the ones who understand that I can't go out on weeknights at the drop of a hat like I used to, and who don't make me feel bad about it. I have new friends too – friends with babies. Friends like A and C and E, who I talked sleep-loss with in the early months, and who I now moan to about practicalities. These new friends have become important. The old ones seem bemused by them.

uture

I only fully appreciate the commitment that is having a baby who will become a child when I think about the future. For the first time ever, I know what we will be doing in four years' time, because in four years' time N will need to go to school. So we will be living somewhere near a school that is decent enough for us to want to send him to it. We will almost certainly not be living in a tent in the desert, or on the bank of an Indian river. Some people manage to do things differently, but I don't think I will be one of them. I believe in ordinary childhoods because I had one of my own.

One evening, aged nearly nine months, N starts saying 'G'. He greets me at the door when I come home from work with a 'G'. I change his nappy and he says 'G'. We play a bit and he says 'G, G, G.' This is the first proper letter sound he has ever made and he is proud of it. It has come from nowhere. It wasn't as though he was practising; the sound has just formed, perfect on his lips. Sometimes he varies 'G' with '*Grrr.*' '*Grrr,*' he says, '*Grrr.*' I phone my mother later that evening. She has been looking after him for the day. I accuse her of spending the day saying 'Grandma' to him over and over. 'I certainly did not,' she says, defensively. 'I did say Ma, Ma, Ma a lot though.' These Gs and Grrs are his own idea. He can't get enough of them. The next morning he wakes up and is still doing it, only now he is rolling his Rs separately too. '*Rrrrrrrrrr,*' he trills, like a Frenchman in his cot. '*Rrrrrrrrrr,*' he rolls. He is enjoying himself. Already, these noises are a form of self-expression. I am here. I can do this.

I can make these noises on my own. 'G, G, G, G, G.' Over the coming weeks, the G becomes 'Ga', a proper baby 'Ga'. And sometimes 'Ga' becomes 'A-ga'. '*Ga,*' he says, and looks up at me, immediately, for approval, pleased with himself. '*Ga, ga, ga.*' He concentrates, and pronounces each letter perfectly, precisely. Sometimes, I sing a corrupted version of 'I Am the Walrus' to him. 'G g g chew, g g g g chew,' I sing to him, and he answers with a big, delighted-with-himself smile and a very pronounced 'G' every time.

Games

When he is seven-and-a-bit months, N starts to enjoy his first game. You clap your hands together, one two three, one two three, and he reaches out: he wants to clap your hands, too. Pat-pat-pat, he goes, keeping the same rhythm, his tiny hand on my enormous-looking one. Pat-pat-pat. He has not yet worked out he can do the same thing with his own two hands. Counting is another game he has just started to enjoy. I do it in the bath, when it's time to come out. 'One.' He'll look up, big eyes staring at me from deep in the tub, curious, expectant. 'Two.' He'll start to smile. 'Three.' He knows what's coming next. His smile widens. 'And out comes the boy,' I call, and lift him up and out of the tub, and lay him on his towel, head in his hood. At other times I hold him up in front of my face and speak out a countdown, like they do in the class I take him to. 'Five. Four. Three.' He watches my mouth carefully, for clues, serious but smiling.

'Two. One.' And then I swing him in the air. He laughs. Babies at this age are supposed to like playing peekaboo, but N doesn't seem to understand the point of it. I hide my face under a cloth or towel and then whip it off and shout, 'Peekaboo,' like the books tell you to, but usually he looks confused, or uninterested. He does like the flaps in his books that open to reveal small, round, blobby babies' faces. But it seems to be the faces he responds to, not the fact of their having once been hidden.

He is, however, interested in football. He has a green ball with bumps all over it – a 'sensory ball', the shop called it poshly – and his favourite game, after clapping, is to pat the ball back at me when I roll it to him across the floor. He is like a seated, stationary tennis player, taking great swipes at it with his hand as a racket. His aim is precise. He studies the ball as it rolls away from him across the floorboards, smiles when I trap it under my foot and kick it gently back towards him. He reaches out for it, brings it under control with the palm of his hand, and then rolls it back in my direction. Eight months ago he was not even born, and now he understands how to control a rolling ball, how to make it do what he wants. I am not sure how this happened.

erms

Once you have a baby, germs start to play a major role in your life. You spend the morning with a mother and her baby who has a cold and the next day your baby has a cold, too. You secretly curse the mother with the snotty baby who has given your baby a cold, because now your baby is up all night, which means you are too. Once your baby is being looked after by other people along with other babies, germs are outside your control. For the first few months that they share a nanny, N and M take it in turns to give each other various illnesses: the winter vomiting bug, endless colds, a chesty cough. There is a new illness each month, which usually starts out with one of us thinking and therefore telling the other one it is just 'teeth', because everything is 'teeth' until it turns out to be something else. When one baby comes down with it, the other gets it a few days later. A and I take it in turns to apologise to each other, to say it's fine, really it is.

Getting married (when pregnant)

I read somewhere that ten per cent of women in this country are pregnant when they get married. I was one of them: I was seven months pregnant at our wedding. It was as much about N, as yet unborn, as it was about us. We had been together for ten years, but I liked the idea of being married when I was in labour. I liked the thought that I could say 'my husband' or that D could say 'my wife' to the doctors and midwives while I was trying to give birth. I thought those phrases would carry more weight if things were going wrong. I bought a size fourteen dress a few weeks before-hand and hoped it would still fit on the day. We left buying wedding rings until the last minute in case my fingers swelled up in the final weeks (they did; D and I ended up swapping wedding rings).

I felt a bit ridiculous on the actual day. I remember shouting at D to go and get my posy of flowers. I told him I wouldn't walk into the register office without it. I felt big, vulnerable, and I needed it for protection. The ceremony was quick and much nicer than I had imagined. A friend read Sylvia Plath's 'You're'. My father cried and then got bossy with D's sister, who was taking the photos, to try and cover up his tears. The registrar found it impossible to pronounce D's (Romanian) middle name. She made it sound like a type of food poisoning (we had second thoughts about passing the name on to N). At the meal afterwards I could sit down throughout: a luxury. Later, in the pub, I did a bit of standing and a tiny bit of drinking. Everyone else did a lot of drinking. I had to drag D away at the end of the night, back to our hotel, where we had been upgraded to a suite that was as huge as my now massive bulk deserved. The next day we caught a train to the Gare du Nord and the man at the baggage scan told me not to lift my suitcase off the conveyor belt myself but to wait for my husband to do it. I opened my mouth to correct him and then closed it again. In Paris I checked the bars and restaurants for prams and buggies. There were hardly any. The absence of baby paraphernalia would be made up for as soon as we got home: we were due to embark on our weekend-long NCT course, which was meant to teach us how to have a baby.

Getting out (of the house) with a baby

In the first six or so weeks of N's life, trying to leave the house feels like trying to climb Everest. The process takes hours. In order to go outside I need to have a shower and get dressed, so I wait until N is asleep in his Moses basket before racing into the shower. I don't wash my hair because it would take too long. I do clean my teeth. Then I rush back into the bedroom to check he is still asleep – he is – and I start to get dressed. This in itself is challenging, as none of my old clothes fit. Also, I need shirts that button all the way down for feeding and I have only two of these and they are both in the wash. My maternity jeans won't stay up and my old jeans won't go on. I settle for maternity jeans with a belt, but then N wakes up before I can find a top, and he's crying so I pick him up and hold him. I try to shush him but he needs feeding so I collapse back into the bedroom chair. I feed him for about twenty minutes and then he falls asleep so I lay him down in his basket again. I find a top and put it on. I am dressed! N is asleep but if we're to go out he needs to be clean and dressed too, so, probably stupidly, I carry him over to his changing table and I change his nappy. He is still asleep while I do this, and he is still asleep when I button his babygro back up. I carry him downstairs, but then decide that because it's only April I need to put a coat on him, so I carry him back upstairs, still asleep, and take a coat out of his chest of drawers. I discover that it is hard to put the coat on him while he is sleeping. There is something rigid about how the coat is made:

the arms stick out like they are saluting something on their own. As I am trying to get N's right arm into its sleeve, he wakes up, screaming. He screams and screams and he does it for so long that I decide I have to feed him again. I take the half-put-on coat off him and carry him downstairs to the sofa and undo my top and start feeding him. Half an hour later he falls asleep again. I sit there with him sleeping on me and wonder how long I should stay like this. For about ten minutes I don't move. Then I remind myself that I really do want to leave the house today. (I have made a promise to myself that I will try and leave the house once a day.) I decide to lay him down, still sleeping, in his buggy. The moment I lift him off my chest he cries, so I hold him again, and then he calms down and stares around the room a bit, and then he fills his nappy. So I take him back upstairs to the changing table and take his babygro off, because that is dirty too, and take his nappy off and change it, and dress him in a clean babygro. I carry him back downstairs and put his coat on and he cries. I lay him in his buggy and he screams. I decide I will have to take him out of the buggy again because he is bright red with rage. I lift him out and hold him and walk up and down the living room, up and down, up and down, until he falls asleep. I carry him back to the hall. I lower him down towards the buggy as gently and slowly as my arms will let me. I slide my arms out gradually from under him and, miraculously, he sleeps on. I put my own coat on. I push the buggy towards the front door. I open it. I marvel at the light, the sky, as the front door opens. I carry the buggy down the steps so as not to risk waking the still sleeping N.

I stagger like a zombie through the park, surrounded by other staggering zombies pushing prams.

Goodnight Moon

At nearly twelve months, N is obsessed with a board book called *Goodnight Moon*. It is a strange, old-fashioned book, apparently a classic in America. Half the pages are in black and white, the other half are green with details in bright orange. The pictures in green, set in the great green room, have lots going on in them; there is much more happening on the page than in any modern baby's book. By contrast, the black and white pictures have hardly anything happening in them at all. N likes to touch the bright orange balloon that hangs in the green room on the first page. Always, always, he has to touch the tiny black and white mouse who has a whole page to himself. The mouse is stranded in the middle of the page inside a small grey circle and N strokes it. I wonder if he likes this small mouse because he himself is so small compared to the rest of the world. He presses the mouse with his index finger and looks at me, as if to say: 'mouse, yes.' On the evenings when N is refusing to go to sleep in his cot, when he is lying there in the dark, angry, and shouting to come out, I carry him back downstairs. I sit him on my lap and I read him *Goodnight Moon*. The rhythm of the words is very soothing. 'Goodnight clocks/And goodnight socks.' N turns the pages and touches the mouse and the balloon and when we get to the end he wants it again.

We read it again and then usually again. After about ten minutes, N starts to yawn. This is my cue. The comb and the brush and the bowl full of mush have done their thing. I carry N back up to his cot. I lay him down. He is calm. He clutches one hand on top of the other as he always does when he is ready to go to sleep. I wind up his musical clock and leave the room. The baby monitor is quiet. At some point, he falls asleep.

When N wakes in the middle of the night with teeth pain, D and I take it in turns to recite *Goodnight Moon* to him. We lay him between us in the bed and we speak it out as slowly and calmly as we can. We recite the lines we can remember, and then we make up new ones. 'Goodnight Gordon Brown/Goodnight London Town.' We carry on, murmuring the words, until at least one of the three of us falls asleep.

Grabbing

We have a film of N aged three months, grabbing for the first time. He is lying on the sofa in a stripy top and he has his eye on my big, shiny red plastic ring. He extends his arm, concentrating hard, fingers outstretched. I start to lower the ring towards his hand and he strains towards it. His arms are jerking like a hyperactive puppet with the effort. His eyes are fixated on the ring. What is it? He wants it. He can almost touch it. The arm is still upright, reaching out, jerking, a puppet nearly off the wires now. I lower the ring a tiny bit further. And then the fingers move back in a pincer grip, almost in slow motion, and they reach out and, finally, amazingly, close shut on the red plastic ring. I let go of it and he has it all to himself now; he has claimed it. He is victorious and he grins and waves the ring around in his fist for a few moments. This is the start of something. It is the start of N saying 'I want' and going about getting it. I feel unbelievably proud of this, his first grabbing of an object. Then he drops it.

Grandparents

Now that I have N, I discover I need my parents in a way that I have not needed them for about fifteen years.

In the beginning, I resist the idea of having my parents more in my life again. Without asking, my mother books the week off work when N is due. She imagines she will be coming to live with us when he is born. I have to break the news to her that I don't want her here that first week. I tell her I might prefer it if she comes to stay after D has gone back to work. She takes it quite well.

When I am in labour, waiting for D's mother to arrive to drive us to the hospital, I suddenly decide I need to speak to my mother. Things are getting serious now. The contractions are strong and fast and I am starting to get scared. I think I can feel the baby moving down and I'm worried it's all happening too soon. My mother, I think, will help calm me down. It is eight in the morning and I call the house between contractions. No one picks up. She is already at work. This is not her fault; she has no idea that I have been in labour all night. But while the phone is ringing and ringing in their empty house, a part of me wishes I hadn't told her to stay away, wishes she was here. Already the boundaries are shifting and N is not even here yet.

N is born at ten to eight that evening. My parents are the first people we call to tell the news. They drive down to see N the next day. We are all still in the hospital. I am walking back from the doctor's station, where N has had his check-up, when I see my parents in the waiting area through the narrow windows in the swing doors. I am holding N to my chest. They see us coming and both leap up from their chairs. I try to indicate to them that our room is near where they are waiting, that we are coming through to them, to stay there, but realise they can't hold themselves back a moment longer. They charge through the double doors towards us. I am wearing pink bed socks and they are slippery on the hospital floor. Back in our room, my parents take it in turns to hold N and photograph each other holding him. When we are finally discharged, they drive us all home. Then, as we've asked them to, they leave us to it.

I become increasingly aware of the starring role my parents have in my life again when N is a few months old. He is gradually becoming more focused on other people and he seems interested in my parents when they come to see him. Perhaps it's because they pay him so much attention, talking to him, looking at him properly in the way babies like to be looked at. He smiles and smiles at my mother. I realise N and my parents are going to have their own relationship, outside any relationship I have with them.

My parents start to be some of the easiest people to be around. When I'm with them, I don't need to pretend that there is anything more interesting in life than N. They know and I know that there isn't. N gives us something important in common again. My mother wants to know everything he is up to: his teeth, his sleep, his eating. She wants all the details.

My parents come into their own on my first day back at work. It is a day I have been dreading since N was born. My mother and father come down together; my father takes the day off work. I leave the house before they arrive, leaving D in charge of the handover, because I cannot face it. All day at work I sit and wonder what they are doing. I find it almost impossible to stay at my desk. I call my mother as often as I dare. At the end of the day I rush home. N is sitting on the sofa next to my mother. He is playing with his plastic activity table, spinning the stripy ball and smiling. He is kicking his feet out in front of him and looks perfectly content, as though this has been a day like any other. My mother makes me tea and brings out some cake she has bought. My father is in the kitchen cooking us dinner. I am blown away by their kindness, staggered that they should know exactly the right things to do.

Since N has been born I have been learning how to be a mother, but it strikes me now that I have also been learning how to be a daughter again.

Growth spurts

When I picked N up this morning he felt heavier than he did yesterday. Babies do not grow gradually, they do it all at once. One afternoon you look at them and they are suddenly about a foot taller than they were before lunch. In the early days, growth spurts are exhausting. Instead of getting an hour-long break between feeds, I'd get ten minutes. This would happen every few weeks, and any extra neediness or crankiness on N's part would be blamed (by me) on a growth spurt and more milk given. In those weeks I felt as though I never left the sofa or deckchair. (I realise there are worse places to be stuck.) I'd eat more than usual, cramming in cake and fruit and bread, anything I could find. It was easy to imagine it was all going to N, even though clearly it wasn't: it was sitting on my hips, my stomach. New bits of me appeared that I'd never had before. With each growth spurt N experienced, I went through one of my own.

As babies get older, you don't always notice them needing to eat more food, but you do notice bits of them growing overnight. A baby you saw only three days ago will suddenly look chubbier, or longer and thinner, or have bigger hands.

aircut

Now that N is one he needs a haircut. It is getting in his eyes and is thick and bushy on top. It really does need cutting, but I don't want to do it, and I don't want anyone else to do it either. People are starting to mistake him for a girl.

Hands

Aged two-and-a-bit months, N is lying in his Moses basket, perfectly still, apart from one hand, which he is opening and closing in front of his face, like a bird opening and closing its wings. He is staring at his hand as it opens and closes, opens and closes. 'I have a hand,' he seems to be saying. 'Just look at it. My own hand.'

Aged eight months, N stares at my hand. He looks down at his own much smaller hand. He holds it up against mine and looks. 'The same,' he seems to be saying. 'The same.'

As he gets older, N uses his hands to communicate. Pointing is his thing. It comes as a relief to him. We have been thinking about trying what the books call baby sign language, but then N learns to point, which makes it redundant. He can now point at the food he wants – a bit of banana maybe, followed by a bit of stuff from the jar, and then a bit of that baby rice cake. He points at each thing in front of him on the table. Eating becomes a slow, many-course process. He is so excited about pointing that he starts to become imperious. He sees his favourite toy – the red wooden bus – at the other end of the room. Instead of shuffling over to it, which takes some considerable effort, he points at it and looks at me and stays where he is. He sticks out an index finger or, more usually, twists his whole hand towards it, as though asking a question. This is his sign for 'get the bus for me', and sometimes I do. But often I do not; often I laugh at him and tell him to get it himself, and he gets very cross. I worry that if I bring him what he wants every time, he will expect life always to be this way. So I restrain myself, even though he is only a year old, even though he is still experimenting with this new way of telling me exactly what it is he wants.

ead

Of all the things newborns do, it is the way they bob their heads that makes them seem most tiny and fragile. When I lift the just-born N to my shoulder, his head goes bob,

bob, bob, bob, bob against me, and with his eyes closed and his head moving like this he is like a new kitten or a baby lamb. The bobbing means he needs something from me: he is hungry. It makes him seem almost unbearably vulnerable. His head bobs and nuzzles against my neck, and with this motion I realise that we are more animal than I thought we were. It is a sweet and innocent reflex. I am not sure when it stops, but one day I realise he doesn't do it anymore. Perhaps it is when he is three months, or four. And he no longer eats his hands to tell me he's hungry. I wonder whether he has stopped because I now know what he wants without his needing to make these signs. Now I know that there is a hungry cry, and I know that there is a different, high-pitched cry for wind or pain. I miss the head-bobbing once I realise it has gone. But there are compensations in the head department. When N is nearly ten months his head starts to smell of shortbread, as though he has just raided the tin.

Holding your baby

Newborn babies need to be held *all the time*. They need to hear your heart beat, to feel your warmth, to smell your familiar smell. Put down, put aside, they scream and panic. They are terrified to be alone. For the first three months, I spent all my waking hours holding N. I was either feeding him as I held him or just holding him. Like all mothers of newborns, I ate my meals holding him and tried not to spill food on his head. I drank my coffee holding him and tried not to spill that on his head either. I held him while I was cooking. Sometimes, when I really needed to get things done, I put him in a sling in order to empty the dishwasher or peg the washing out. I remember feeling elated when, one morning, when he was about two months old, I managed to change the bed with him lying in his Moses basket, awake, in the same room. When I had finished, without him crying, I felt as though I had just achieved the most extraordinary thing. I didn't know if there would ever be a time again when I could change the bed and it not feel like a miracle. I had no idea how long his needing to be held all the time would go on. I felt panicky because I didn't know how I would ever get anything done in my life ever again. Not even the washing up.

I am not sure now how long this stage goes on for: you don't notice it ending. But I know that a few months on, I wasn't holding N every waking minute of every day. After a while I could put him under the baby gym and he would swipe at the wooden rings and beads for a few minutes at a time. I would rush round like crazy in those minutes, trying to get everything done – the washing on, the kettle boiled, the bottles in the steriliser. There was never quite enough time. And then, as summer came and he turned three, four months old, N would lie out in the garden under a tree and stare up at the leaves, stare up at his own hands against the sky. The leaves and his hands would keep him occupied. I could sit in a chair next to him and read a book, if I could manage to keep my eyes off him long enough to make sense of the words on the page. Just sitting on my own in a chair was a liberation. In those moments out in the garden, the process of our separation had, I suppose, begun.

Holidays

Holidays with a baby are not what they used to be. The fact that you are on holiday does not mean that your baby doesn't need to be lifted out of his cot at six or six-thirty in the morning. It does not mean that he won't straight-away need changing and dressing if his nappy is leaky at this ungodly hour. It does not mean, as the day goes on, that he won't need his nappy changing at various intervals, that he won't need feeding breakfast, lunch and dinner in rapid succession and probably a few snacks in between. He will still need settling down for his naps once or twice a day; he will need to be bathed and dressed and got ready for bed every evening. He will still need to be played with most of the rest of the time. He will still need watching closely (even more closely than at home) to make sure he doesn't trap his fingers in the bedroom door or fall down the stone steps that lead straight off the kitchen in the house where you are holidaying. There will be no lie-ins. There will be a lot less lolling around reading books. There will be less daytime drinking. At some point during your holiday you will remark to yourself that it might have been more restful to have stayed at work.

Hospital bag

As my due date gets closer, I become obsessed with my hospital bag. I pack it two weeks before N is due and then I unpack it and repack it almost every day after that. I can hardly walk past this bag without opening it and looking inside. It sits there, dark and squat on the landing outside the bedroom door, waiting. A bag stuffed with babygros and tiny hats and all sorts of equipment that I will apparently be needing for myself. I have packed the bag according to a list given to me by the hospital, supplemented with a list from my friend J. I can't imagine what some of the things are supposed to be for. The breast shields make sense, but I am not looking forward to using them. The maternity bra is just plain ugly. The nipple cream makes me nervous. The maternity pads are properly disturbing. J says I should take a water spray for labour, and I've packed one because I do everything she tells me to, but I try not to imagine what I will end up doing with it. She also says I need pyjamas (not a nightie, she says, there will be blood) so I have them too: men's from M&S, size ginormous and with the requisite buttons ('button-front everything from now on', she advises). I have packed a box of paracetamol in accordance with hospital instructions, which strikes me as stupid, because from everything I've heard about labour, paracetamol is going to be no help whatsoever. There are clothes for me to wear after the birth. There are bed socks. I am worried about the lack of dressing gown. I have packed dried apricots and dried mango slices to eat in labour. At the last minute I add my iPod. It starts to become difficult to close the zip of the bag. I wonder if we need to go out and buy a bigger bag, or perhaps just forget the bag and hire a trailer instead. My hospital notes sit importantly on top of the pile. This is a bag full of hope (the tiny clothes) and full of terror (those damned pads).

H ospital visits (when pregnant)

I have always hated hospitals, but I looked forward to antenatal check-ups. Waiting for ages on the hard chairs in the waiting room, fetching water from the water cooler, clutching the big white book of notes was all part of it. Pregnancy is, after all, one long waiting room, and the hanging around felt appropriate. I liked looking at all the other pregnant women. I was interested in their shoes. Many of them, I noticed, wore trainers, which struck me as sensible in the circumstances. A few were still in heels. I felt sorry for those who had children in tow – I'm not sure why, probably because quite a few of them looked tired, and not as thrilled to be here as I was. For them it was not a novelty.

The first midwife check-up at twelve weeks seemed to validate the fact of my pregnancy. Until then, I had been playing it cool, trying to remember to say 'If all goes well … ' before even daring to mention the word 'baby'. It was about not tempting fate, not counting one's chickens, and various clichés like that; suddenly they no longer felt like clichés, but like very urgent truths. The midwife at that first appointment seemed relaxed and confident: 'When you come here to have your baby,' she said, 'in six months' time … ' For the first time, as she handed me leaflets about what to eat and what not to, I allowed myself to acknowledge that it was actually going to happen. I had been nervous about this first appointment, imagining such humiliations as stirrups and gloved hands, but there was none of that. (No one wants to look at you down there when you're pregnant.) When we left I felt like I had passed some kind of initiation ceremony. I was different now; I was going to have a baby. D and I both celebrated by going back to our offices and sitting down at our desks and doing some work.

We were back at the hospital once a month after that. I started to feel almost comfortable being there. But not so comfortable that I could bring myself to look when I passed the labour ward on my way up or down the stairs. I dreaded hearing screams. The visits were to the old hospital, before the maternity ward was moved to the new building, and it was very Victorian Gothic. Even looking at the scratched metal beds standing empty in the corridors with their handles on the sides was terrifying. I hated the thought I'd be screaming on one of those beds at the end of all this. The only way to stay calm about pregnancy was not to think about labour. At one of my appointments I followed a very pregnant woman walking heavily up the stairs. She seemed to be in labour. She was wearing a pair of tracksuit bottoms and was climbing the stairs very slowly and breathing in an exaggerated way. Her partner was following equally slowly behind her. He was wearing a bum bag presumably packed with urgent supplies and he looked excited and important all at once. The woman didn't look excited, she looked as white as one of the bleached hospital sheets. But I took heart from the fact that she wasn't screaming and that at least she could still walk.

When the maternity hospital moved to the new building, there was no walking past the corridors of the labour ward on your way up or down. Sensibly, they kept all of that off-limits; everything was hidden away behind doors with special access codes. There were no beds with handles on view to indicate the tortures ahead. The new building was brighter, shinier, with coloured transfers on the windows, presumably to suggest something cheerier than the bloody agony of labour that the Victorian place seemed to align itself with. The midwives hated the new hospital building, they said. It was too big and nothing worked properly yet – hardly reassuring.

We continued to go to the appointments – for the weighing, the blood tests, for them to listen to the baby's heartbeat. I was surprised that it was as simple as this: a fifteen-minute check-up and then back out into the world to get on with things. My dental check-ups took much longer. But with each appointment I felt I was getting closer to something. Each time I went my stomach was that bit larger. I felt like a ticking egg-timer (a weeble-shaped egg-timer), getting louder and louder with each hospital visit that went by.

ouse

Anyone who needs to live in a tidy house should avoid having a baby. Coming in through the front door of our house, this is how it goes. There is a buggy in the hall that you have to squeeze by. Past that, down the stairs, the double buggy for when M is here is folded up on the floor of the study. The baby rucksack and the folded-up travel cot live under the desk. When we built this study, D gave me a picture of the cover of Virginia Woolf's *A Room of One's Own*. The plan had been for it to hang on the wall there, since that was where I was aiming to get things done. We ended up putting the picture in the living room, and the study is now a dumping ground. When I type or read, I do it on the sofa in the basement next to N when he is playing on his mat, or up in the living room next to him when he is playing with blocks. Studying, typing, reading, are certainly not things done in a room of my own.

Down past the not-study, into the basement, there are two high chairs at the kitchen table: N's chair and a spare for M. If it is the middle of the day, the floor in the basement will be covered in N's toys: a plastic piano that doubles up as a baby walker; a wooden xylophone; a cloth tool box; a set of plastic cups that slot one inside the other. Also down here is a changing mat with a baby gym standing over it, because N's changing table is two floors away, which is a long way when you are holding a baby whose nappy has exploded.

Up the stairs to the middle floor and into the living

room, there is another play mat and a box on wheels full of toys (the toys are probably all over the floor up here too). A baby bouncer hangs in the double doorway between the two rooms. If M has been today, the travel cot will be in the middle of the room, and the double buggy will be up here too: the room looks more like a nursery than part of our house.

In the bathroom, the rack that goes across the bath, which used to contain soap and a sponge, is now stuffed full with two plastic dolphins, two frog washing cloths, plastic cups for pouring water and plastic books. There is a stick stacked with plastic hoops with a giraffe's head at the top suctioned to the side of the bath tub.

On the landing outside our bedroom are piles of maternity clothes, baby clothes and other things N has grown out of. They are waiting to go up into the loft, and they have so far had a long wait. N's room is full of his things: his cot, chest of drawers, his changing table, a trunk full of toys he is still too young for, his wooden ark, his flying wooden bird which we haven't yet got round to hanging from the ceiling. Our bedroom, in comparison to all the other rooms in the house, doesn't look too bad. N's things are confined to the space under our bed: the zip-lock bags full of more clothes he has grown out of.

The house is littered with tiny socks that keep getting separated from each other; they are scattered about the place like confetti. Little fur boots and various outdoor jackets hang about the hall.

It is not as though we don't try to keep things tidy. This

invasion of things is something we spend much of our time at home trying to contain. It is a battle we are always losing. Even people who have children walk into our house these days and do a double take.

Hug (N's first attempts)

At ten months, N has learned how to hug properly. If I pick him up in the middle of the night when his teeth hurt, or first thing in the morning when he is sleepy, he will push his arms around my neck and squeeze them tight. He is trying to hug me. It feels like a koala bear holding tight. When he does it in the middle of the night I don't even mind that it is three a.m. and I am up, swaying in the dark, trying to soothe him back to sleep. Because this hug he has just learned to give feels like a secret, stolen thing.

I *(as in, myself)*

Now that I have N, I am still myself, but I am different too. I have learned to be more domestic. I spend my time differently. Today, my day off, we went for a walk in the park so that N could have a nap and I could have a coffee. We walked home via the toy shop to buy presents for the twins next door whose mother lends N all the clothes they have just grown out of. After that we went to the greengrocers to buy fruit and vegetables to make more purée. When we got home I put N in his high chair and cooked him cubes of puréed parsnip, sweet potato and carrot from the batch in the freezer that I'd made the week before. After lunch I let him play, and then I put him down in his cot to sleep and wondered about writing Christmas cards. This is the sort of day I remember my own mother having when I was child. Gentle, calm, practical. It is not the sort of day I ever used to have myself. Now that he is nine months old, N needs to have a proper lunch at the proper time, ideally sitting in a high chair because that way more goes in his mouth and less down his front. If possible, it's best for him to have his after-lunch sleep in a cot, because these days he sleeps better and longer in a cot than in his buggy. I submit to these new realities. I am falling into the routine of motherhood, into the meal-making, the cot-settling, the toy-tidying. When he was newborn and there was no food to bother with and he could sleep anywhere, we were mobile and busy and impressed ourselves with what we could do. Now that there are cubes of frozen food and messy high chairs, it all feels more fixed. As I work out how to use this new equipment, I feel myself becoming a mother for the long haul.

llness

Aged nearly a year, N gets properly ill for the first time. He has a hacking cough like an old man and his nose is running all over his face. The cough, when it is bad, makes him sick, and it hurts. During the day, he is too exhausted and in too much pain to play. He wants to be held and carried; he doesn't know what to do with himself. His eyes are red-rimmed and keep closing, even when he is sitting up. He can't hold himself awake properly. He looks like a tiny drunk. He can't stay awake in the day and he can't sleep at night. He just wants to rest his head on my shoulder and sleep like that, all night, and when I try to put him back in his cot he wakes up and looks at me as though I have betrayed him. Then he starts crying again. I get up three or more times in the night to hold him and sway him back to sleep. I fall asleep on the sofa in his room, holding him at three a.m., and when I wake up he is still lying with his head on my shoulder, arms round my neck. He is fragile and needy again. Really, he is always fragile and needy – he is a baby – but when he is well he tries hard to pretend not to be. He is not pretending now.

I take him to the doctor, who listens to his chest and says he has a virus. I tell him I have taken his temperature once and that he is hot, and he tells me not to take it any more. He thinks I am a neurotic mother, but I don't think I am being neurotic about this, because I am actually very calm, I just want N to get better. The doctor prints out a prescription for antibiotics and N and I go straight to the supermarket chemist. The supermarket is usually one of N's favourite places – there is so much to look at on the shelves – but today he struggles to focus on the packets and tins all lined up brightly there for him, fights to keep his eyes from closing again. I take the day off work because I do not want to leave him; D takes the following day off. I am home for the next four days. I will not leave him until he is better. I give him spoonfuls of vile-smelling antibiotics, which he gulps down greedily. D and I start living on food from the freezer, as we did when N was a newborn. Gradually, as the days go by, N's cough seems to rack his body less. He can sit alone and play for a few minutes at a time. Then one night he sleeps through for the first time in ages. D and I wake in the morning having had eight hours' uninterrupted sleep. Or rather D's sleep has been uninterrupted, whereas I have been up in the night checking, assuming that because he is not waking as normal, N is dead. He is not dead, he has just remembered how to sleep, so I stumble back to bed and try sleeping too. N's chest is full of phlegm and he sounds like a drowning sailor, wheezing loudly in the next-door room, and when I do finally drift off again I dream I am on a bridge that is becoming overwhelmed with water and is sinking fast. But then it's the morning, and N is talking and babbling in his cot. For the first time in ages he isn't crying.

nternet

The internet is important when you are home all day with a baby. It is like a life raft thrown out onto the sea of empty time while everyone else is busy at work. It helps you feel as though you have not completely lost your grip on what is happening in the outside world. It also tempts you to spend money. I find myself staring mindlessly at mail order baby clothes pages, wondering what it is exactly that I need to have delivered. I don't know why I am doing this. It seems I find it relaxing in some peculiar way. Unlike a baby, the internet is very biddable. A couple of clicks and you can get it to do exactly what you want. Email helps keep me sane on the long maternity-leave afternoons, when it is easy to assume the world has forgotten about me. I hold N with one arm and tap away at the keyboard with the other, pinging messages out into the void, checking constantly for replies. Hello, I am still here, my emails are saying. Please don't forget about me. All the other new mothers I know are constantly emailing too. I pity women who had babies before email and the internet.

Interviewing

When N is five months old I begin worrying about going back to work. Now that he is here I am no longer sure about the nursery we have signed him up for. In itself it seems hard to fault, but there are several problems with it. The biggest problem is that it is two miles from our house and not on a direct bus route. It is, however, a nice cycle ride down the canal from where we live. When we signed him up, I pictured us taking N there on the back of one of our bikes, happy in a baby seat. But now I can't imagine the idea of cycling with him through the London traffic on the way to the traffic-free canal. Back then I also had no idea how long it takes to leave the house with a baby. What with getting out of the front door, and then the detour via the nursery, first on a bus and then on foot, and the dropping off and settling, and the walking and then getting on another bus, I estimate that getting to work each day would take at least an hour and a half. This is too much for one four-mile journey. And then, of course, there would be the pick-up and the journey home. It would be a three-hour round trip. I am also getting strange flashbacks about the baby room at the nursery, which I didn't pay much attention to at the time – the toddlers were more interesting – and I have a vague recollection of lolling, helpless babies. All things considered, I am going off the nursery plan. So when A, a woman who lives nearby with a baby, M, who is the same age as N, tells me she is thinking of hiring a nanny, I ask her whether she might want to share. A likes the idea. Nannies are expensive, but a shared nanny is about the same price as a nursery place, which means we would at least still be able to afford to eat. A puts an advert on the internet.

This is how I find myself interviewing strangers who wish to care for my baby. (I realise I am lucky to have had this luxury.) I sit there on A's sofa holding five-month-old N, wondering what on earth I am doing. It feels like a game. When the first candidate doesn't show up, I am relieved. Maybe no one will want the job; maybe I won't be able to leave N after all. But then H, the second candidate, does arrive and she is neat and calm and professional-seeming. She talks about what she thinks babies want and how she likes to look after them (she likes to stay at home for a good part of the day; she likes to do one trip out in the buggy a day; she likes to play with them a lot; she likes to create a calm environment for them). After she leaves, A and I agree she is the one. When we call her references they tell us we would be mad not to hire her, and so we do. She will start in three months' time and will look after both babies together. It is perfect. I should be thrilled, but instead I try to forget all about it.

eans

I stop buying myself clothes after N is born. We are broke, for one thing, and I look so bad in everything. If I want to treat myself, I buy tiny clothes for N instead because he looks so good in them. N is ten months old when I accept that I need to buy new jeans, but I can't face it. I can't face knowing that my thighs, my backside, will still look enormous, however expensive the jeans I buy. I know this is vanity: I have never really thought of myself as vain before, but it seems I am. I can't face the stick-thin sales assistants; can't face having to explain myself to them. 'I've just had a baby,' I will tell them, apologetically, when I know, but they don't, that the baby is almost a year old now and therefore no longer an excuse for the spare tyre that still hangs around my middle and on top of my hips. I used to live in jeans, but it is possible that the new me just may not wear them. I console myself that dresses are at least very quick and easy to put on.

icking

I'm not sure how many months pregnant I was when I first felt N kick, but I remember where I was and what it felt like. I was at my desk at work. I felt a small fluttering on my left-hand side. I laughed. I wasn't sure. Then I felt it again and I laughed again and clutched my hand over the spot. There it was, N's first message out: 'I am here. Kick. Look. I am here.' 'Hello,' I may have said out loud at my desk, 'Hello, hello.' That kick was reassurance, it was certainty: there really is a baby in there and he is signalling to me. After that he kicked a lot. He kicked just after breakfast, lunch and dinner – high on sugar or carbohydrates, with new energy to burn off. He kicked after coffee when I started drinking it again. He kicked in the morning – though not too early – to let me know he was awake too. He kicked on the train to work when I was getting squashed by people, as if to say, 'Oy, you lot, give us some room here.' He was still in the night; he slept when I slept.

Out in the world, N still kicks a lot. From the age of about two months he shows us he is happy by lying on his back and kicking his legs wildly. Aged nine months, he still does this when he hears songs he knows, or when he goes down in his cot for his morning nap, and he kicks his legs in his high chair when he is enjoying his food. When I carry him upstairs, facing out, he bicycles his legs madly and laughs and laughs. At ten months, he still kicks on his back, but when he sits up his new thing is drumming his heels. Drum, drum, drum on the kitchen floor. This is an upright way of using his legs and showing us he is happy. Drum, drum, drum. Before he can speak words, he talks with his feet.

abour

Labour creeps up on me by stealth: a silent ambush.

As the first contractions start and I'm not sure if they really are contractions, I decide that it is very important to start re-covering the dining room chairs, right now, this evening. It is nine p.m., and I am four days past my due date. I'm getting occasional cramps, and I am down on my hands and knees, pinning and cutting fabric and stapling it to a wooden frame. (I have never tried to re-cover a chair in my life before, so, in retrospect, it should seem strange that I'm starting now.)

I get one cushion covered, but the cramps are starting to feel like they might be contractions, and it's hard to concentrate on cutting the fabric for the next cushion in a straight line. I give up on the rest of the chairs – there are five more to go. TV might be a good idea, I think. Earlier, I walked to the rental shop and picked up a subtitled film with impressive-sounding reviews all over the cover. I put it in the DVD player and it appears to be a documentary about the decline of the French fishing industry. The subtitles seem very small. The film is very slow and I find it hard to follow. After half an hour D asks if we can turn it off, and I agree. We put on a Bridget Jones film instead. This is more like it. I sit and roll on my birthing ball and laugh at Bridget in her silly see-through-in-the-rain dress. D starts to time the contractions with a timer he's found on the internet. 'Go,' I shout as a contraction comes on, and he hits the space bar on the laptop like a dog out of the starting gate at Walthamstow Stadium. 'Stop', I yell, as the contraction dies away, and D smacks the space bar again, quick as a flash. D tells me, because he is monitoring these things, that they are proper contractions: they are regular and getting longer and closer together.

After Bridget Jones I put on *Sex and the City*, because it too is fluffy and distracting. I keep dropping off to sleep now, waking up to flashes of Miranda and her baby shower, Carrie and Big having another bust-up. At some point I go upstairs to bed, and drift in and out of sleep for I'm not sure how long. I put on the TENS machine we've rented and it feels buzzy and weird, but I like having the button to press when a contraction comes: it gives me something to do.

It is about seven-thirty in the morning when I suddenly decide that I need to go to the hospital NOW. I need to be there this instant. The contractions are coming fast and full: I can't speak when they come; I can't get up off my hands and knees. D disappears somewhere, calling his mother to come and collect us, packing up our things. It feels as if he is gone for hours and I can't call him because I can't speak and I start to panic. It feels as if the baby is about to come out, right here in the bedroom. When D's mother arrives she wants to talk to me, but I can't talk. I climb into her car clutching a cushion I have taken from our bed. I am in my pyjamas and a pair of wool-lined boots and I have the TENS machine in one hand. I am dimly aware of the neighbour opposite staring at me. I kneel on the back seat and clutch the head rest. I notice children on their way to school peering at me as we drive up the road.

It is a quarter to nine now and the middle of rush hour. D and his mother have a disagreement about the best route to drive. I am filled with panic. I have the strong urge to push. D's mother flings the car over the speed bumps. We go up and down in the back, up and down. I grip the head rest harder. I am in so much pain now I can hardly see. I have no idea where we are, but I know that D and his mother are still arguing about the best way to go, and I am also aware that the car spends more time stuck in traffic than it does moving towards the hospital. I feel something slimy and wet sliding down my leg and I have no idea what it is. I think I am going to have the baby in the car.

When we pull up outside the hospital I am so relieved I nearly cry. A porter takes us up in the lift. I kneel down on all fours in the reception area of the birthing centre and grab hold of a chair. I am terrified that they might send me home again, which is what they threatened to do when D phoned to say we were coming. I focus on holding onto the chair, and barely speak to the midwife, who is asking me questions. Not talking seems to do the trick: she tells us she will get us settled in a room, and once she has led us to one I get down on all fours again, leaning up against a low bed this time. I tell her many, many times how happy I am to be here, and I mean it.

After a while she gives me an internal examination. Getting onto my back for it is excruciating and takes ages. I can hardly bear to do it. The midwife, A, says I am eight centimetres dilated, and seems happy with that. I am just relieved that we are now definitely, definitely allowed to stay.

A is busy with another labour, so she drafts a second midwife in to look after me. He is an ex-banker and I like him a lot. 'You'll have the baby by three,' he tells me confidently. It is ten a.m. I have five hours to go. I wonder if I can make it. He fills up the enormous bath tub in the middle of the room. I am excited about the prospect of climbing into it. I have always loved baths – but this one seems to take hours to fill up. I realise after some time that the water is only just trickling in. The midwife is trying to spin out my getting into the pool: he is trying to give me something to look forward to.

Finally it is full and I climb in. The contractions are making me want to push, but the midwife tells me not to. He tells me I have to ride over them. I grab onto the side of the pool when one comes and kick my legs out and try to ride it. It is nearly unbearable. I float around in the tub. Between contractions, it is pretty pleasant: I chat with the midwife; the student nurse who is here to watch me give birth brings me sugary tea. When a contraction comes, trying not to push is a nightmare. 'Don't start asking for an epidural,' the midwife tells me. 'You don't need one.'

I have been in the pool for hours when I decide, suddenly, to get out. I heave my bulk out of the water. I am naked from the waist down. The midwife dresses me in a hospital gown (some distant part of me realises I am half-naked and enormous, that he is trying to help preserve my dignity). When I look over at the clock it says ten past three. Ten past three and no baby. I haven't even started to push yet. I remember his advice on the epidural. 'How difficult would it be to get an epidural now?' I ask. He pulls out a stool and tells me to sit on it and try a bit of pushing. I do. The pushing feels so much better than trying to ride the contractions. Now that I am pushing, it feels as though I might be able to make it to the end of this thing. I squat and I push and then I get up and walk in the corridors and push. I grab hold of the handrail and I bear down on it and push and push. A midwife comes by and asks if I'm meant to be doing this and does my own midwife know and D says yes. I walk up and down the corridors for hours, stopping to hang off the handrail when a contraction comes. A is back from delivering her other baby and she takes over again. When she checks the baby's heart rate it is raised. She takes it again a few minutes later and it has calmed down – so have I.

When I stop walking the corridors and go back to my room the clock says it is past seven. 'If you can get the baby down a bit further, I can give you an episiotomy,' A says. 'And then you should be able to have him here.' I do not want to go down to the labour ward. I want to have this baby here and I want to have him soon. I push and push but very little is happening. I am not really having contractions any more, but I keep on pushing anyway because I want to get this baby out. I had never imagined I would be so desperate for such a barbaric-sounding procedure, but I am. I am pushing and pushing in the hope of getting one.

A gets me on my back, which is an agonising process, and then she makes the cut. I feel nothing when she does it apart from relief. I hope the fact she has cut me means we are nearly there. There is another midwife here now with A and she is trying to coax the baby out of me. It is not coming, though, it is not coming. A and the new midwife can't seem to tell that I'm not really having contractions any more, and that I'm just pushing whenever it feels as though one might start but doesn't.

On the floor in front of me, A picks up the phone to the labour ward. She wants a doctor to come up and look at me. She says doctors don't usually come to the birthing centre: they expect you to go down to them. I am not listening to the conversation because I am concentrating on trying to push, but then I hear her say: 'If you don't come, there's a good chance she'll have the baby in the lift.' She puts the phone down and shakes her head. They will not come up, I have to go down, and there will be no way back here after that. 'This is what happened to my mother,' I hear myself moan. In the end they used forceps on her, because her contractions had stopped. Throughout my pregnancy I have been worried by my mother's stories of her long labour with me which ended so badly. I am suddenly terrified of what they might do to me on the labour ward. I have the idea I will have to start all over again if I go down there and I don't think I will make it through. I feel such an urge to be left alone, not to be meddled with. I push and push as A calls a porter and asks for a trolley to take me to the labour ward. Someone tells me the trolley is waiting at the door for me, but I hardly hear them. Suddenly, my contractions have come back, and I am pushing for real again. I can feel the baby starting to move down. And then a huge contraction comes over me, and I am so glad. When I look down I see that A is placing a clean towel on my lap, which I suppose means she thinks something is about to happen. I close my eyes and bear down hard again. I tell D to push down on my shoulders to help me and he pushes and I push. Suddenly I am in agony. The baby's head is there. It is unbearable. I scream: 'Fuck, fuck.' A tells me to pant and I pant like a mad dog. I am going crazy with the pain. Then another contraction, and I feel the baby slipping down and out. I have to tell myself to stop screaming and open my eyes because they are still closed against the pain, and I force myself to open them and look down at the towel. A is putting a tiny, red baby in my lap. He is not crying and he has his hands up by his face. He is blinking in the light like a baby animal. He is surprised to be here, and I am surprised he is here too, finally, and now I am the one who is crying.

aughing

N's first laugh comes early. He is about three months old. He is lying on his play mat on his stomach (he hates lying on his stomach) and I am waving a white stuffed bear in front of him. I waggle the bear and make him say, 'Hello N,' in a way I could never have imagined myself doing before. N stares at the bear jiggling around in front of him. Then he chuckles. This is a complete surprise, to him as well as me.

'What did you say?'

I jiggle the bear again, wondering if I have imagined it. I dance it about all over the place, but there is no more chuckling.

A few weeks on he is giggling all the time. He laughs when he is lying on his back and I bicycle his legs. D says, 'Ma ma ma ma ma, da da da da da,' and N gets a fit of the giggles. His giggle is satisfying and infectious. I always feel good – about me, about N – when I make him laugh (which is not hard), and I can see that other people around him do too.

As he gets older, other babies start to make him laugh almost uncontrollably. When M arrives in the mornings, N laughs and laughs at him as he crawls all over our basement floor. He thinks crawling is hysterical. It doesn't occur to him that it is something he might want to do too. Crawling is something M does for N's amusement.

When N laughs at him, my father says his laugh should be bottled and given to people who are sad. I hadn't expected there to be so much laughing.

aundry

Babies create an avalanche of laundry. Early on, the pile of washing they create each week weighs more than they do. In the first weeks, we had to change N's clothes two or three times a day. It would go like this: cardigan is suddenly covered in sick, comes off; on closer inspection the babygro, while not covered in sick, has been affected by a leaking nappy, so that comes off too. Once that is removed, the vest underneath it is also discovered to be dirty, so off that comes as well. N is at this point screaming his head off (newborns hate to be naked). The urgent task is to get him dressed again; to shove his stiff, resistant arms as gently as possible (while at the same time applying some sort of force in order to make him bend the rigidly stuck-out things just a little bit) into a clean babygro, and after that, the misery (for N, for me) of having to do it all over again with another layer. Often, at this stage, a new cardigan is felt to be excessive (by me); it is spring after all, and N is very cross at having his arms yanked about. The dirty items get thrown into the bucket to soak along with all the other shit- and vomit-stained things. They float together in a soapy soup. It is a new bucket that I have bought just for this purpose. It is bright pink and cheerful, which is just as well, as there is little else that is cheerful about having to do this much washing every day.

As N gets older, our markers of what we consider dirty change. A little bit of leakage on the bottom edge of a vest is tolerated, for instance, so long as it touches nappy and not skin (we usually apply the last bit of that rule, but not always; it depends if we're out, where changing is a nightmare). A bit of leakage onto the inside of the baby sleeping bag is mopped up as best as possible with a wipe so that the bag can be used again that night (they take ages to dry; we only have two, and the other one is usually in the pile of laundry when we need it). Shit, gradually, becomes less of a problem stain-wise, or maybe it's just that we get less fussy about it. Then at six months the problem becomes food. The issue is with N's clothes, but also now our own. The purée goes everywhere: in his hair, in his ears, all over my trousers, all over his high chair. It is acceptable for N to sit around in purée-covered clothes all day – he is a baby who is learning to eat; people are understanding about these things. It is, however, less acceptable for his parents to sit around in cauliflower- and carrot-covered outfits, or turn up to the office in them. So while we can get away with one outfit change for N on a good day, our own clothes have to be changed more often. The laundry pile is teetering, while the pink bucket hasn't seen so much action since those very first weeks. I start to swab myself down after feeding N, in the hope of limiting the damage, but there is always some butternut squash or apple purée on his fingers that I have somehow missed and that gets smeared all over my skirt/trousers/dress moments after I have returned triumphant from sponging myself.

I am fighting a losing battle with the laundry, I realise. Better to resign myself to the fact that we are going to be doing one, perhaps two, loads of washing every day for the next eighteen years or more, and then hanging it all up and folding it and putting it away. I prefer not to think about how many future hours of my life I will be dedicating to laundry. I draw the line at ironing; I'm sure that if, in some mad moment, I decided to take it up, I'd never be able to leave the house again.

Leaving your baby

In the beginning I find it impossible to leave N. It starts on the maternity ward in the hospital. I discover that I do not like the idea of going to the bathroom to have a shower and leaving N on his own in the plastic cot. I am frightened someone will steal him. All the other babies have been tagged with electronic devices that will, apparently, go off if anyone tries to take a baby off the ward. N, for some reason, has not been tagged. They have overlooked him. I hate the idea of him being tagged like a piece of clothing, but not as much as I hate the idea of him being the only baby who is not tagged. If they tag the babies, they must think they need to. I feel certain N is at risk.

It is early morning on the ward and I really, really need to go to the loo. D is not yet here and things are getting desperate. N is asleep in his cot. I look around the ward for potential babynappers. I decide I have no choice but to run for it. I pull the curtains closed around our cubicle, so that N is hidden. I rush to the bathroom as fast as I can, clutching my phone – in case I get locked in, so that I can call the hospital switchboard, tell someone to watch N while they are getting me out. I am as fast in the bathroom as I can be. I wash my hands in a panic. I am overcome with relief when I discover that I am not locked in. I almost run back to my cubicle. I am full of dread as I reach the curtains; I actually pause before I open them because I am suddenly certain that N won't be there when I do. I am shaking. I know that he has been stolen. I yank back the curtains. N is lying in his see-through plastic cot, just as I left him. I approach the cot. Now the fact that he hasn't moved is worrying me. Someone could have smothered him in the minutes I was gone. It would only take a moment. I stand and watch him for signs of life. He is so still and so silent. I see his chest rise and fall microscopically and am overcome with relief. I have left him and he has survived. It is terrifying, his being out in the world now. He is no longer inside me, he is out here for the taking. I need to guard him at all times. I ring the bell for a midwife, and when she comes I ask her if she can please tag my baby.

During this, our second stay in hospital, I leave him properly for the first time. I am on the hospital feeding cycle. I feel like a cow in a shed; I am being milked non-stop. In my half an hour between milking times, I decide to take a walk down Tottenham Court Road. I need to get out of this place, so hot and airless and full of angry midwives. I wander out of the hospital and into the street. I am wearing tracksuit bottoms and wool-lined boots. The fresh air shocks me, like a slap round the face. I am in a daze. I forget to look out for cars when crossing the road and nearly get run over. I am confused and feel as though I am doing something illegal, like a prisoner who has broken out of jail. I feel the strong urge to go back, but I tell myself to make the most of these thirty minutes. I need this air. I need a few moments to myself. I have had none since the birth, after all. But my mind keeps racing back to N, who is asleep in his cot being watched over by D and who suddenly seems a long way away. By the time I get to the stationery shop I have been heading for, he is half the length of Tottenham Court Road away. It is too far. I feel as though there is a piece of invisible string tied to my waist, yanking me back towards him. I hurriedly pick out some cards – 'congratulations on your baby' cards for some of our NCT 'classmates' who are also, it turns out, on the ward – and rush back. N is asleep and D is staring into his cot and I sit down next to him and stare too. He has not noticed my absence, but I have felt it keenly.

Back home, a few days later, I try leaving him again. We need vegetables and I volunteer to get them. I leave N at home with D. The shop is a five-minute walk away. Going across the churchyard on my own feels wrong. It is like I have forgotten to take my arm or leg with me.

N is six months old before D and I decide we will try properly going out without him, together. D is used to leaving him because he goes to work, but then N is with me. I am never apart from him. He has never been apart from both of us at the same time. D's sister has theatre tickets for a Saturday matinee that she can't use; can D and I take them off her hands? We talk about it and in the end agree we will. We drive N over to D's mother's house. We sit with him there for a few minutes. I have read in a book that you shouldn't make the handover too sudden, but the traffic was bad on the way over and we are late. He seems happy enough so we leave. We give her detailed instructions about naps, precise times for milk. We drive towards the theatre. The traffic is terrible so we abandon the car in the middle of town and get on the tube. We look at each other inside the carriage. We are on our own riding on the tube and N is not with us. We are doing what we used to do before he was born and it feels strange. Because we ditched the car, we arrive a few minutes early. There is time for a drink in the bar. We sit down at a table with a glass of wine each and there is no baby in a buggy to check on. We clink glasses. D texts his mother to ask if everything is OK. She texts back: everything is fine. We go into the auditorium. They search our bags as we go in. This makes me nervous. Is there some sort of terrorist threat we don't know about? I imagine a hostage situation – how will I get back to N? We take our seats and I try to put the bag search out of my head.

The play starts. I surprise myself by becoming absorbed in it. D is enjoying it too; he is laughing beside me. In the interval we leave the building as quickly as we can. Out in the light, D calls his mother. She says N is having a nap. I am amazed that not only is everything fine, but we are managing to enjoy the play as well. We go back in and the second half is even better than the first. We clap enthusiastically at the end but leave as promptly as we can. We leap on the tube, eager to get back, congratulating ourselves for thinking to abandon the car as we did. We collect the car and drive back, and when we pull up outside D's mother's I can hear N screaming from the street. D rings the bell and there is no answer and the screaming is very loud and I want to break the door down. D finds his key and lets us in and I follow the screaming into the living room. N is sitting on the sofa wearing only his nappy and D's mother is sitting next to him. He is screaming in a way I have never heard him scream before. He is shouting: '*agggh, agggh, agggh*'. He is bright red and naked apart from the nappy. I pick him up and hold him and my heart is pounding like mad. I try to breathe calmly because I want N to be calm. D's mother says she has taken his clothes off because he was too hot. I walk up and down in front of the fireplace holding N against my shoulder and he starts to quieten. He is shuddering with relief now; the cries are just whimpers. I see a bottle of milk on the table. I lie N in my lap and offer him the bottle. He glugs at it greedily. I try hard not to cry.

In the car on the way home, N is asleep in his car seat, peaceful, but I am livid with rage on his behalf. Mostly, I am furious at myself for leaving him. When we get home, I sit and hold N the rest of the night. He has forgotten the afternoon but I have not. I tell D we will not be going out again.

anuals

Before N is born, we read the books that tell us how we are supposed to look after a baby. Neither of us knows anything at all about babies. I have never had any interest in them up until this point. My mother murmurs things about instincts kicking in, which sounds reassuring, and I hope she is right. I have hardly even held a baby before, apart from when I visited J and G in hospital. So D and I do what we always do when we feel underinformed and go to a bookshop. We buy a book that someone has told us we absolutely must have, called *Baby Secrets: How to Know Your Baby's Needs*. When we get home we worry that one book will not be enough so we go round to a friend's house and borrow another, and then, just to be safe, we go to the local library and borrow a few more. Among the titles: *Secrets of the Baby Whisperer: How to Calm, Connect and Communicate with Your Baby* and *What to Expect the First Year*. Some sound worryingly like self-help books, others like instruction manuals for cars. I never thought I would have books with titles like these in the house. In the last weeks before the birth, D and I sit up in bed at night reading them.

According to the books, babies love routines. It is never too early to get your baby started on one. It is, in fact, possible to get a strict schedule up and running as soon as you get back from hospital. New babies should be fed every two and a half to three hours, and not for more than half an hour at a time. If your baby falls asleep during feeding, you are encouraged to tickle his chin or feet or to blow on his face to wake him up. After a baby has eaten, he or she should be discouraged from going straight to sleep, unless it is the middle of the night. He or she should lie around awake or, if old enough, 'play' for a while instead. Only after an interval of time has passed should he or she then go to sleep. During the day, this should happen in a 'rocker chair', which is the correct place for naps according to one book. Swaddling the baby in a sheet or blanket is also a good idea. Once the baby is asleep, you, the parent, are allowed to eat, or drink tea, or go to the loo, or put the laundry on, or, in the words of one book, have some 'you time'. In the evenings, a baby should have a bath and be put to bed upstairs in a cot or a Moses basket.

One book has a system for grading babies. Babies can be spirited babies or touchy babies or grumpy babies or angel babies or textbook babies, according to how they feed, how they sleep, how they play, what their mood is like. The books are full of warnings. Never cuddle your baby to sleep (never let your baby fall asleep on you at all). Do not be tempted to feed your baby to sleep either. A baby needs to learn how to get him or herself off to sleep; to do it with milk is cheating. Do not allow your baby to sleep in your bed – this is bad for everyone. The books are very strict. I worry we are not going to be up to the task ahead.

After N is born, we look at the books again and they seem to be describing an alternative universe to the one we are inhabiting now. We are feeding N every two and a half hours because the hospital has told us to. But his feeds take three times longer than the books suggest they should. N falls asleep while he is feeding because it takes so long, which is also strictly forbidden by the books. I sit with him asleep on me in the way they say I shouldn't, or I lay him down, asleep, in his Moses basket, also in the way they say I shouldn't. When N gets stomach ache in the night, D brings him into bed with us and lies N on his chest, which seems to calm him. This is all wrong according to the books, but it is the only way N can sleep in these early weeks, which means it is the only way any of us can sleep. Because of the books, D and I feel guilty about bringing N into our bed, even though it is clearly what he wants. Haunted by their reprimands, I sometimes wake up with a start, worried N has fallen out of bed, that he is on the floor, under the covers, suffocating somewhere, but he never is. He is sleeping peacefully on D or sleeping in his basket if D has put him back.

The books say it is important to introduce regular bath times early on to establish a good bedtime routine. We are scared of giving N a bath; water is so slippery and N is so wriggly. Each evening we tell ourselves we will do it. N is five or six weeks old before we are finally brave enough to put him in a tub of water. We bath him and we feed him and we put him in his Moses basket like the books tell us to, but N cries and cries. He needs to feed some more, he needs to sit on me or D, he will not lie on his own. I spend the first post-bath evening sitting on the sofa with N dozing on my front and feeding from time to time, which is the way I have spent every other evening since he was born.

After a while, we stop looking at the books. They only make us feel like failures.

Maternity leave

I am frightened of going on maternity leave. I have arranged to finish work two weeks before N is due. As the date approaches, I wish I had suggested staying another week, or even waiting until the start of labour, since the hospital is right opposite my office. I don't know what I am going to do with myself when I am not at work. I know that once it arrives a baby will keep me busy, but I have a fear of long, empty days and going mad with loneliness. I have it in my head that I will take six months off work; six months is of course a luxury that many women do not get, but still it looms up at me as something endless, threatening.

The first week I am on leave, I check my work email constantly. I also do all the things I imagine you are supposed to do before you have a baby: I get my hair cut, I have lunch with friends, I even get my first (and possibly last) pedicure.

I keep myself busy. But then it dawns on me that I probably need to get bored before the baby will come, so one day I experiment and do nothing but read a book and re-cover a chair, and that evening it all starts.

D has six weeks' paternity leave, starting the day N is born. We are fortunate. Even in England, this much time is unusual. Most men get two weeks off work. I spend the first two weeks of N's life in and out of hospital, first because N has lost too much weight, and then because my blood pressure goes sky high. If D had any other job, he would be going back to work just as N and I are being discharged from our third stay in hospital. But he stays home and looks after us for another month, and it comes to seem normal him being around too.

Maternity leave as I have imagined it – being on my own with the baby – starts when D goes back to work. I have been nervous about the inevitability of this. I have no plans for the first day N and I are finally on our own together. The weather is good – it is early May – so I sit in the garden and feed him. I try to read while I am doing this, but for some reason this is difficult, so I give up and just sit. Feeding him takes most of the morning because he keeps falling asleep. At lunchtime I decide we will try and get out of the house, something we have not done on our own so far. I change his nappy and his babygro and strap him into the buggy and lift it down the steps. I roll him in the direction of the park and he quickly falls asleep. On the way to the park we pass a café with tables outside and I realise I have not eaten today because I have been holding N all morning, so I sit down and order a sandwich. I eat the sandwich and then order a coffee and N sleeps on in the buggy. I feel pretty pleased about what is happening. N sleeps and I sit at my café table and wish I had bought a paper. I start to feel like a lady of leisure. Then I look at my watch and realise N will need feeding again soon, and that this will be best done at home since it takes so long, so I buggy him back to the house. I spend the rest of the afternoon feeding him again in the garden. At five o'clock it starts to feel cool, so we go inside. D will not be back for another hour and a half. N seems to think he needs more milk, so I put the *Sex and the City* DVD into the machine and sit on the sofa and carry on feeding him, while Carrie and Samantha go about their babyless lives on-screen. When D gets home I am onto my third episode and N is asleep on me. I have survived my first full day on my own. It hasn't been too bad.

But I am not sure if I can have this sort of day every day of every week for the next six months. At some point I will need to see other people, or at least have a conversation with someone. And as most of the people I know are at work during the week, this means I will need to spend time with other mothers. Since I do not know any other mothers, this means I will need to meet some. I have had an email about a tea that is happening in my area for women with new babies. I have made a note that this tea is happening today, my second day alone with N. I hate meeting new people. I tell myself I must go. I stand on the doorstep of the house where it is meant to be happening with N in the buggy dressed in his smartest cardigan and ring the bell. I am full of dread. Nobody answers. The house looks shut up and silent. I check my email on my phone and discover I have got the wrong day. I turn the buggy for home with a sense of relief.

On my third day of being alone with N, some of my NCT 'classmates' – the ones I learned how to have a baby with – have arranged to meet in a café. We are supposed to be there at ten a.m.. I discover, as I am trying to get ready to leave the house, that it is very difficult to be out anywhere by ten a.m. when you have a new baby. Even with D staying behind, so that he will be late for work, and helping to pack the nappy bag and set the buggy up and get N dressed, it is going to be difficult to make it. Because I have to get showered and dressed too, and while I am supposed to be doing this, N is deciding he wants feeding, so I end up sitting dripping wet in the bedroom chair, feeding him, watching the minutes tick by on the clock. Finally I manage to dress myself and put N in his buggy, but he howls and howls for more food. I sink back into another chair to feed him. My heart is fluttering oddly in my chest: this may be a response to the blood pressure tablets, or perhaps to my anxiety about being unable to get out of the house. The weird heartbeat is making me feel dizzy and light-headed. I discover that I am crying. I wonder if this is how postnatal depression starts. D hovers by the front door looking worried. He is late for work but I am crying. I tell him to go, we will be fine. He hovers some more and then I tell him again to leave, so he does.

N feeds and feeds and then he falls asleep, so I lay him in his buggy and carry him down the front steps and into the world. We are outside and it is still only quarter to ten! I am suddenly feeling much better – the relief of being outside. We buggy to the bus stop. I have not taken the buggy on a bus on my own yet, but when the bus pulls up I lift the buggy on just fine and feel a disproportionate sense of achievement. N wakes up as we drive off and he seems happy. He likes the movement. He sits and looks around him, at the strip lights overhead, at the world sliding by outside the window. I text D: WE R ON THE BUS! I feel triumphant. After a while we get off and I wheel N towards the café. My watch says ten a.m. I can't believe it: we are even going to be on time. I feel like I have just won the London Marathon, I am so proud of myself.

Two women from the class are already there when we arrive. They look pale and ghost-like. We hug one another, like soldiers just returned from battle. We have met only once since the childbirth classes, and that was before any of us had babies. We sit at a table as our babies sleep in their buggies or their slings and we each order a strong coffee. We talk about milk and breasts and tiredness and pain and labour. Gradually, my heart, which has been jumping about all morning, starts to beat more normally. One by one our babies cry to be fed and so we feed them, sitting there together. We order lunch and eat one-handed while our babies are feeding or sleeping on us. I realise that I am now part of one of those groups of mothers and babies that I used to go out of my way to avoid in public places. The pre-baby me found these gangs annoying (with their buggies and sense of entitlement – they took up so much room!) and just a little bit pathetic. And now here I am and I suddenly get the point. They are about such basic things: having some company and being able to drink a cup of coffee – even coffee isn't always possible when you are home alone with a baby.

I catch the bus home hours later. We have arranged to meet again next week. I have something in my diary other than empty pages. I feel lighter because of it.

As the weeks go by I develop a routine. On Mondays I stay at home with N or go for a walk in the park. On Tuesdays I take N to the nearby mother and baby yoga class then meet some local mothers for coffee. On Wednesdays I take N to be weighed at the baby clinic and, when he is a bit older, I take him to a baby massage class, which he loves. On Thursdays I meet my NCT group. On Fridays I stay at home and go to the park again. I have gone crazy for classes because they give structure to our days, but I look forward to the weekends when D is home and I can have a bath in the morning without having to keep leaping out of it, stumbling towards the Moses basket where N has just woken up crying.

I enter things into my diary obsessively, even though all my weeks are similar. Even small commitments must be set down so I can see what lies ahead. I fear the empty diary page, the empty week. It is not that I do not enjoy being with N, but I find it easier to sit and feed him or hold him when there is someone to talk to for at least part of the time. I like pushing him around in his buggy, but sometimes I need to know that I am pushing him towards something rather than just moving around for the sake of it.

emory

Now that I have N I cannot remember what life was like without him. It feels normal that he is here. Except for one moment today. We were at the local baby music class and N was standing on my lap, straight and grown-up-looking at eight months now, and he seemed so solid and child-like that I suddenly couldn't believe he was mine; he felt like someone else's baby. I was so shocked by the feeling that I almost dropped him. I didn't like it. Until that moment he had felt like one of my own limbs. Perhaps in that moment I realised that N is his own person, not a piece of me. Who knows what it was. Whatever, that sensation of not knowing who he was flew off as quickly as it had arrived. And then he was my baby again, and I knew him completely.

iddle of the night

The middle of the night is a lonely place. Ever since I was a child I have had a dread of finding myself awake when everyone else is asleep. At three in the morning it is possible to feel as if you are the only person in the world. When N wakes me around this time to be fed, I put the radio on. Radio 4 has given way to the World Service for the night shift. I have hardly ever listened to it before, but it is comforting to be reminded that there are other people alive still talking about politics in Africa or telling children's stories (which they do, bizarrely, in the small hours). The chattering soothes me as I sit and feed N, hunched over in the dark, D sleeping beside me. Before he went back to work, D would wake up with me, but now he sleeps on. Sometimes I feel so odd in these early hours that, selfishly, I wake him up anyway. Having a baby means you spend more time with yourself in the silence, in the dark. There is no getting away from yourself in these early hours. But at least there is the radio.

idwives

Midwives are vicious. Or my midwives were, anyway. Correction: the midwives I had for my labour and delivery were amazing and extraordinary. It was the ones who came after who were vicious.

The first community midwife who sailed into the house, a large woman with a million bags slung about her person, took one look at N and barked: 'Are you topping up?' I had no idea what she was talking about. My mobile phone credits? My bank account? I asked her to explain. 'Are you giving him formula after breast-feeding, to fill him up?' I told her that I wasn't, that I didn't even know you could do that, and she harrumphed. She weighed him – I think – and asked me if I was feeling depressed and then left.

The one who came after her was worse. 'Your baby has lost too much weight,' she shouted. 'We are going to have to send you back to the hospital. They will probably put feeding tubes into him.' But before we could go to hospital, D had to be packed off to buy a breast pump, bottles and formula. While he was gone, the midwife opened a carton of formula she had on her in case of emergency, poured some into an object that looked like a lid but turned out to be a feeding cup, and then poured it into N. He drank it greedily. I'd been feeding him non-stop, but I'd been doing it all wrong and now he was starving and I hadn't realised.

This midwife stopped N starving and, naturally, I am grateful to her for that. What I am not grateful to her for is the way she treated me. After she had poured the formula down him, she wanted to watch me feed him. She was in a rush. It was Mother's Day (the irony) and her daughter was cooking her lunch and she wanted to be off. She shoved N's head onto my breast, yanked me about this way and that, told me, 'Not like that'. I did my best not to cry from frustration, but also from embarrassment. 'Where has your husband got to with those bottles?' she tutted. 'I am going to have to leave before he gets back at this rate.' Then more tugging and shoving of me and N, before she pronounced, 'I wasn't meant to come here today. You were not on my list. I came here on a feeling. Now I know why. The Lord sent me to save this baby.' She looked down at N with a sad shake of her head. If I had been my usual self that morning, I would probably have asked her to leave. But I wasn't my usual self. I was so unlike my usual self that I was unrecognisable. Instead, I bowed my head, meekly. I had done wrong. I had failed to let my baby thrive. Now he was going to have tubes stuck into him. 'The Lord sent me a message,' the midwife said again, as I did my best to get N latched on properly, while her rough fingers pushed his head up and at me.

When D arrived back from the shops, literally breathless, with the bottles and the pump and the extra cartons of formula, it was like the cavalry had finally come. 'Sterilise it,' she ordered, shoving a bottle at D, 'I haven't got much time.' D ran around the house, sterilising bottles, producing the pump for her inspection. 'Wrong kind,' the midwife pronounced, shaking her head. 'I hope you kept the receipt. You need one with batteries.' Finally, what she judged to be the correct kind of bottle was ready, and she poured in more formula and fed it to N, who gulped it down. Then she handed N and the bottle to me to take over. 'I have to go,' she said. 'Once he has had this bottle, you need to go to the hospital. I will call them and tell them you are on your way.' She punched numbers into a mobile phone. 'I have a re-admission,' she said. 'The baby has lost twelve per cent of his birth weight. I have fed him formula in a cup and now a bottle. They will be with you soon.'

And then she packed up her bags and her mobile phone, which had been ringing off and on throughout her time with us (her daughter, wanting to know when she would be arriving for lunch), and with one final shake of her head and pronouncement of, 'The Lord sent me today to this baby, truly he did,' she was off, leaving me pole-axed on the sofa with a bottle and a baby.

When we arrived at the hospital, we were assessed by a doctor. This doctor, who was sensible and kind, and nothing like the midwife, explained that N had almost certainly been getting some milk from me, but not quite enough. She said that in her view we had turned a corner with the feeding now, and if it had been up to her we could go back home. Her registrar, however, thought it safer that we spend a night on the ward. I asked, would there be feeding tubes where we were going? The midwife had said there would be tubes. The doctor looked shocked and said there would be no tubes, just me feeding him lots. 'Tubes,' she said. 'Whoever gave you that idea?'

As soon as I met the midwife on the ward, I realised she was made of the same stuff as the community midwife. She explained that she was N's midwife, that I would get my own, that her look-out was the baby and not me. She eyed me coolly as she explained this, and then handed me a chart which I was meant to fill in. The regime was that I was meant to breast-feed N every two and a half hours, then top him up (that famous phrase) with formula and then pump whatever milk I had left to increase the supply. 'The whole process should take no more than one hour,' she explained. 'In between, you should sleep.'

I was feeding N sitting up in bed later that evening when she came over. 'You need to drink more water,' she said. 'If you don't drink enough, you won't make enough milk.' I fumbled for the jug on my tray table. I had to lean out of the side of the bed awkwardly to get it, and as I was pouring it, one-handed, because I was holding N with the other hand as he fed, the lid came off and cold water gushed every-where, including onto N as he lay feeding. N was soaked so, naturally, he started crying. 'Look what you've done,' the midwife tutted. 'You'll have to change him, you realise. He's wet through.' Of course I have to change him, I thought, why wouldn't I change him? But I didn't say that. Instead I stammered, like the naughty schoolgirl I clearly was, not a thirty-two-year-old mother who had accidentally upset her hospital water jug: 'Yes, yes, I'll change him.'

This midwife's job was to wake me every two and a half hours so that I could start the feeding cycle all over again; a cycle, I had already discovered, that it was impossible to complete in one hour, but in fact took more like two, leaving me half an hour in every two and a half to go to the loo, wash my hands and get twenty minutes' sleep. At two a.m., the cubicle curtains whipped back. The midwife loomed up at the end of my bed. But I was ready for her. I was sitting up and already feeding – hah! I had decided that I would give her no more excuses to berate me. I'd set my alarm for five to two, so as to be awake and feeding by the time she got to me. I wouldn't give her the satisfaction of waking me. I would beat her. She took one look at me, gave a little 'hmm', and left.

I set about the feeding chart like I was preparing for my university finals all over again. I was careful to tick every box (tick colour of nappy), write down every measurement precisely (millilitres of expressed milk given in a bottle; millilitres of formula given in a bottle; number of minutes spent breast-feeding). I laboured all night over the feeding and that chart. I must have slept for no more than an hour in total. In the morning, I imagined someone would want to look over my feeding log, but no one did. No one looked at it for the rest of the day.

That afternoon, I asked if someone could weigh N. He had fed pretty much non-stop since we'd arrived at the hospital and I felt sure he must have gained weight. I was desperate to get us both home and out of the ward, away from midwives who lurked at the ends of beds, tutting. 'There's no point weighing him yet,' one of them said. 'He won't have gained anything. We won't weigh him until the morning.' I tried to object: 'But the doctor said we would only need to stay one night.'

'We won't weigh him until tomorrow,' the midwife said again. 'You'll be here tonight, too.'

A doctor came and gave N his third heel-prick test, which made him scream again (they had lost the results of the other two, or couldn't read them, they were vague about which it was). At this, I finally gave up and started crying. They had beaten me at last. I wept and wept sitting on top of my hospital bed. As I sat there crying and shuddering, some part of me was dimly aware that I was in hospital opposite my office, where every day I went in composed and efficient. And now here I was, on the same street but in a different life, where I was weeping and useless and out of control.

I wept so much and so loudly that they finally sent the doctor back to talk to me. He explained that though they felt N was fine, they needed to run more tests, and that tomorrow, all being well, we could both go home. The doctor acted as though my tears shocked him. But I'm sure I can't have been the first mother re-admitted onto that ward to break down and cry.

The feeding cycle continued all evening and all night.

The midwife gave up on coming to check me as I was always feeding whenever she arrived, still desperate not to have her catch me napping. When I woke after a ten-minute nap for the four a.m. feed, I lifted N from his see-through cot as usual. He was fast asleep, and suddenly I needed to be fast asleep too. I snuggled down with N on the pillow next to me and drifted in and out of sleep for the next three hours. Whenever I woke up he was there, sleeping calmly in my arms, his head on the pillow beside me. It was blissful to wake up with him next to me. And as I surfaced, groggily, I was aware that I had got my baby back. With all the feeding and the fighting with the midwives and the crying I had lost him for a while, but here, now, I had got him back.

In the morning I lied on the chart (the chart which still nobody had checked) about the four a.m. feed. Early on they weighed him. The midwife who had just come on shift said she couldn't believe how much weight he had gained. We were free to go. We packed up our things and the unread chart and we hailed a cab. The community midwives came every day once we were back home. Their tactic was to turn up unannounced on the doorstep. They made it clear they didn't trust me. They seemed surprised when they weighed N in one of their makeshift slings and each time he had gained weight. I felt it like a victory each time.

other

I am a mother now. I am a baby life-support machine. N is almost a year old, but when he cries out I still leap up from whatever I am doing – relaxing on the sofa, sleeping in bed – and run to him. I am sleep-deprived and often tired, but N needs me now and N comes first. To be a mother is to put yourself second (or, presumably, third or fourth if you have more than one child) without even noticing. I am no longer the most important person in my own life.

Right now it seems N needs me, his mother, more than he needs D. When he wakes in the night screaming with his teeth, he carries on screaming when D holds him, and only stops when I take him. In the early days, when I was breast-feeding, I sometimes felt suffocated by this fact of N needing me most. I would lie in the bath in my half-hour off in the evening and hear him scream out for milk and feel the panic rise up in me. Now I am used to his need. I take it as a given.

Moving

N is eleven months and until now he hasn't been all that interested in crawling, or – indeed – moving in any other way. He has been happy sitting on his mat, reading his books, playing with his toys, going nowhere, just turning in circles on his bottom every now and then when he feels like a change. I have liked it like this. He has been self-contained on his mat, absorbed in his play. I have been able to play with him for a bit and then get on with the things I need to do – the boring things like the washing, peeling potatoes. This week he's suddenly a bit more movey. I am writing emails and N is on his mat in the middle of the room. When I look up he has somehow travelled about half a metre and is sitting in front of the disused iron stove, opening and closing the little drawer at its base. I pick him up and move him back to the middle of the mat. I sit and watch him to see what happens. He stares at the stove and the small drawer. He lunges towards it. He dare not crawl, but he slides for-wards slightly on his bottom and thighs. Then he sits up and grabs hold of the edge of the mat and pulls himself forwards a bit. Then he lunges again, and grabs hold of the bolster that I have put in front of the stove. He holds onto it and uses it to drag himself the rest of the distance, until he is in front of the stove again, opening and closing the little drawer, back where he wants to be.

As the weeks go by, between eleven and twelve months, N learns how to propel himself forwards on his backside. If he wants to go super-fast, he scoots with his hands to get up extra speed. He races to the cupboards in the kitchen and opens and closes them, opens and closes them. He is fascinated by doors. I am scared he will trap his fingers in the cupboard door when he closes it, so I sit next to him the whole time he is doing the opening and closing. He does it for a very long time, which means I end up sitting staring into the kitchen cupboards for a long time too. They are a mess inside: they need clearing out. After the kitchen cupboards, he scoots over to the radiator to play with the valve. I race there and reach it just ahead of him, checking quickly that it is not burning hot. It isn't, so he strokes and twiddles the valve for a while. With this scooting, N has finally found his freedom and I have lost the last shreds of mine. He now decides where to go, what to play with. He is in charge. Now that he can move, nothing interests him for more than about thirty seconds. He is like a speed-dater on acid – moving from his blocks to the coal bucket to the wooden box with letters on it to his *Dear Zoo* book, all in less than a minute. His days are spent racing from one thing to another; mine are spent following him around the kitchen, making sure he doesn't hurt himself on the stove, the oven, the table. My world becomes very low-down; it is shrunken, it is knee-height. I start to feel like Alice after she has drunk the contents of the bottle. The table top, the dresser, tower above me.

With N on the move it is like having a newborn again. It is now hard to leave the room without him. I carry him to the bathroom with me as I did in the early days, though I do it now not because he will be upset to be left alone, but because I worry about the trouble he might get himself into if I leave him. It becomes difficult to get anything done in the hours that he is awake because he is moving fast and needs constant supervision. I start to use the travel cot as a playpen in a desperate attempt to do some of the things I need to do. I fill it with his favourite books and noisy plastic toys and sit him in it. He plays contentedly enough for a while and I take my chance to sort the house out or cook some lunch for us in the twenty minutes or half an hour he is occupied in there. After a while, he starts to paw at the sides of the cot like a caged animal, grizzling to come out. I lift him up and put him down on the floor. He scoots off, towards the open door, thrilled to find it there, starts opening it and then pushing it nearly shut, opening it, pushing it nearly shut. I squat down beside him and tell him to be careful of his fingers. There is no point thinking about all the things I need to do but cannot until the next time he sleeps. Instead I try and coax him away from the door that could hurt him, towards the wooden toys, the books, that sit in useless piles all over the floor.

Music class

Most Fridays I take N to the local baby music class. He starts off shy, sitting back on me, pensive, but as things get going he becomes more and more animated. He's never sure about the first song, 'Heads, Shoulders, Knees and Toes'. He gets a bit more interested when the puppet animals come out. The giant black spider puppet that makes the other babies cower, makes him laugh. He giggles when we get the finger puppets out and the puppet dances on his head, nose, chin. He gets very excited at bubble time, when the shrill teacher parades around with a plastic machine full of washing-up liquid that fills the room with soapy bubbles. He stands up on my lap then, reaching out for the bubbles, cheeks puffed out, super-confident. When the teacher hands him an instrument he can shake it now like the bigger babies. He is becoming a boy.

anny-share

Two days a week, N is with H, the nanny, and with M, the baby we share her with. (The rest of the time our mothers help out.) N spends the day trying to keep up with M as he crawls around the basement. When he is not trying to keep up with him, he is stealing his socks. N seems to like H as much as he likes M. She is calm and patient and we are fortunate to have her. For the first weeks, I was jealous of the fact that it was her, not me, taking N to the park, to the swings; that she was the one lifting him out of his cot when he was all warm and just woken up. It was as though she was an intruder I had mistakenly invited in. But now I am used to the arrangement and glad of her help. I realise this whole set-up is a privilege, but it is one I am grateful for.

appies

Until N is born, I have never changed a nappy. In the first six weeks of N's life, apart from the nights we are in the hospital, D does all the nappies. Since then, it is as if I have been studying for a degree in nappy changing. On average, now he is older, N needs to be changed five times in every twenty-four hours. That means five nappies x 365 days, equals 1825 nappies, but because we changed him a lot more in the early weeks and months, let's round it up to 2000. I estimate that I have personally changed about three-quarters of these nappies. I think I should be awarded some sort of official qualification for all this nappy changing. It gets harder once the baby gets older and wriggly and difficult to pin down.

Nappy accidents

Our most dramatic accident happens on holiday after our car has broken down and we are being dragged along behind an AA van to the local garage, and the car fills with the sound and smell of N filling his nappy. I am up front, trying to steer the car, when D reports from the back that it is all going everywhere. It is, he says in a panicky voice, leaking out of the bottom of N's trousers, and is all over his legs, his feet, the car seat. I shriek at him to wipe up what he can while trying to stay on the road. D dabs and pats and I steer. When we arrive at the garage, D unloads N and undresses him on the bench on the village green. I thank the nice AA man for getting us here and then I go over and start scrubbing the car seat, while D wrestles a naked N into the spare outfit we have, thank God, remembered to pack. Luckily, although it is February, the sun is shining. Lucky for N as he is naked in the middle of the village green, and lucky for me, and especially lucky for D, because were it not for the sun I would almost certainly be in tears about our miserable luck at this particular broken-down-car-on-holiday-with-shit-all-over-the-car-seat-and-the-baby-too moment.

CT classes

NCT classes are a rite of passage for most middle-class parents-to-be. The basic arrangement is that you pay a large sum of money for a few hours of lessons about how to have a baby, in the hope there will be one or two people in the class who you will get on with and be able to spend time with once you have your baby. D and I go to our NCT class straight after coming back from honeymoon. It is on the top floor of a very corporate hotel and is being run by a very sad-looking woman called P who is wearing a denim pinafore dress. I am troubled by this pinafore dress because P is not pregnant, and in my own enormous state I cannot see why any non-pregnant woman would choose to wear an item of clothing like this. (I briefly wonder if P perhaps wishes she were pregnant, and if that is why she is wearing it and why she looks so sad.)

P tells us she has four children and she looks completely shattered by the experience. It looks like she should be at home having a lie-down rather than instructing ten sets of parents-to-be about the realities of childbirth and beyond. It looks like she doesn't want to be here in this hotel, and a glance around the room confirms that none of her students do either. She perks up when she starts to get out some of the props she has brought with her, like the plastic pelvis with the baby doll you are supposed to shove through to simulate birth. She proudly unpacks the pair of old tights and the multiple tins of tomatoes and baked beans and pine-apple chunks she has brought with her in one of her many shopping bags. We are instructed to pass the tights around the room and we take it in turns to slip a full tin down one of the legs. Once the tights are bulging and bursting with the tins we have stuffed down them, overstretched so that their feet drag on the ground, P explains that what is happening to this pair of tights is what is happening to our uteruses right now. She says that at this stage, our babies, plus all the extra blood and fluid we're carrying, weigh as much as this stack of tins. We are told to pass the tights around some more. They are indeed very heavy. Some of the men swing them about a bit. I notice the women in the group do not do any swinging; they pass the tights on quickly as if they are very hot potatoes. I start to feel sick whenever I look at the circling tights. For her talk on Caesareans, a subject I am especially keen to hear about, P brings out a Lego operating theatre, complete with anaesthetist, surgeon and midwife.

She saves her most exciting props for the final session,

which is all about how to care for a baby once it is here. She hands out ten identical plastic baby dolls, each dressed in its own real nappy, and she giggles as she does so. She says she has a surprise in store for us, and she can hardly contain her excitement. And we do indeed all have a surprise in store. Because when we take off the baby dolls' nappies we discover that, underneath, the baby doll bottoms are all covered in Marmite. I imagine P, at home, perhaps with the help of her children, dunking her finger in a jar of Marmite and carefully smearing the stuff over the plastic backside of each doll in turn. Some of my classmates seem to be enjoying all this as much as P clearly is. I just keep thinking about the money I have spent on this class and the fact that I really could have done with being able to spend it on other things, like clothes for our baby, or a cot.

Neurotic parents

Before we had N, D and I were scornful of parents of babies. They all seemed so neurotic. We had a bad experience with a couple we went to stay with a few months before N was born. Their flat was full of baby equipment. There was hardly anywhere to sit because all the furniture was buried under stuff of one sort or another. The pram was in the middle of the living room. When we did find somewhere to sit, we couldn't see or talk to each other over it. The couple played with or carried or talked about their baby every hour of the day, even when he was asleep. They told us they had not read a single book in the eight months since he was born. They told us we should get ready to have our lives turned upside down. There would be no books where we were going, they said. D and I raised our eyebrows at each other silently, behind the pram. When we went out to dinner, one or both of them kept leaving the restaurant with the baby because he would not settle. It was true that he wasn't asleep, but he wasn't crying either. Surely their anxiety was excessive. He seemed quite happy in his pram. But it was evening, he was supposed to be asleep, so out they would keep wheeling him, creak, creak, creak, in the hope that rolling him around a bit outside might 'send him off'. The presence of the baby got to be boring, because it was so unrelaxing, what with his parents fussing and fretting over him so much. When we finally left their flat and drove home, we vowed we would not become like them. It is terrible to write it, but when we left, I felt we had been liberated.

Of course, now that N is here, I realise we are just as neurotic as they were (and presumably still are; we haven't seen them in a while). Except we have been able to read books. Since we can't go out, we do get a lot of reading done.

Newborns

Newborn babies are only half in the world. They are still more animal than human. They are like small frogs – squat, splayed out on their mothers or fathers, or flat on their backs as they sleep, arms up like road-kill. They can suck and they can grip a finger insistently and they can cry and they can turn bright red with wind and pain. They are often asleep. They look at the world with round, wide eyes, but they don't really see it. A newborn baby will stare at the top of your head instead of your face (the contrast is better at the hairline, making it easier for them to see). Your own newborn is infinitely amazing, tiny and vulnerable. He is without question the most beautiful thing you have ever seen. Someone else's newborn is inert, out of it, and often quite red and ugly.

Women with older children will clamour to hold your newborn. They will cradle him and coo over him and threaten not to give him back, and it doesn't always look like they are joking. Their yearning for your newborn is in fact a yearning to be back with their own children just born. They aren't longing to be doing all the hard stuff that goes with it – the night feeds, or changing a million nappies – but to be back marvelling at their own newly arrived baby, still not fully formed, still really only half there, and full of possibility.

Nine months

N is about to be nine months old. Soon he will have been out in the world for as long as he was getting ready to be in it. He is in the world more and more each day. Recently, hugs from me have become things to wriggle out of, to strain away from. Hug him too long and he will start to whine and fret. I can't help but be sad about this, but I know that babies are wriggling away from you from the very moment they are born.

ostalgia

I am nostalgic about every moment with N. Now, while he still hasn't learned to walk, aged one, I am already nostalgic about this time of him shuffling about, because I realise that in weeks or months, he will be up on his feet and the shuffling will be gone for ever. He will have become something else: he will have become – that terror-inducing word – a toddler. This is why we have so many photos of him – hundreds of him in his first weeks and months – and a few films, too. They are a frantic attempt to fix the moment. So is writing all this.

N is only one, he is still a baby, but already I have become one of those women who look into the prams of newborns. I feel envious of the mothers pushing their newborns about, just as I used to see other women envy me while I pushed the weeks-old N. I am not sure what it is I envy. Perhaps it is the shock of that new love. I still have it, of course, but I am used to it now. In the early days and weeks, I would sit on the sofa holding N and just stare at him. I was made motionless by love (and by feeding). It would be hard to go on living normally while being constantly confronted by the full shock of that love. It would be hard to go to the shops or the office and take any of it seriously.

I miss the newborn N, but I love this N – this four-toothed boy who likes to pull everything out of the kitchen cupboard and sometimes put it back again. I have always been a nostalgic person. Having N has made me more so. The nostalgia, I realise, is all part of the love.

ffice

When N is six months old, I go into the office to talk about my return to work. I do not take N with me. I don't want to be one of those women who bring their babies into the office unnecessarily. And I don't want the people I work with to catch me out in baby talk. So N stays with his grandmother while I go into the office in a new pair of huge black trousers I have bought specially in an attempt to look smart and professional. I had hoped the black trousers and black top were slimming, but apparently not, because I catch one of the women in the office who has not had a baby looking at my stomach. I imagine she thinks I am pregnant again.

The office is very quiet. People move around in near-silence and sit and stare at computer screens. I walk past my own office but do not look in. I do not want to see my desk, my chair, my computer, waiting there for me. I go straight into my boss's office. I am impressed – just as I was when I was interviewed for this job – by the view he has from here. It is as though I am being interviewed all over again, not because of anything my boss says – he is relaxed and welcoming and wants to know all about N – but because I feel I no longer know this place and need to justify what I am doing sitting here.

I tell him that I am looking forward to coming back, that I am looking forward to getting stuck in to the work again. 'Stuck in' are the words I use. I ask him if he will let me come back four days a week rather than five. I ask if I can do one of those days from home. He seems ready to agree to all this right here at the table, so long as I am prepared to take the one-fifth pay cut that goes with it. I leave the office feeling dazed because I have got what I came for: a four-day week. I have also agreed to a return date. I will be back in November, when N will be almost eight months old. It is longer than I had expected to be away before he was born, but, now that I have him, it feels surprisingly soon.

I rush back to pick N up from his grandmother's house. I used to walk this route from work to hers, but today – because N is there and I have been deprived of him for more than an hour – I catch the bus to save time. I scoop him up when I get there. I try to forget about the office, about the promises I have made.

Other people's (tiny) babies

When N is eleven months old, some friends come round with their eight-week-old baby. She is tiny, curled up in her car seat, and then tiny and curled up on them when they lift her out of it. N is robust and grinning in his bouncer. He looks suddenly older, boy-like, next to this newborn scrap. My friend asks me if I want to hold the baby and I say yes. Before I do I run upstairs and wash my hands: she is so fragile-looking and I am suddenly paranoid about damaging her. I take her and she is as light as a bag of sugar. I had forgotten how little new babies are. She sits on my chest, all furled up, just as N used to. Now his back alone is the length of this whole baby. She snuffles and grunts against my shoulder like a small animal. Instinctively, I fall into a rocking motion. I rock and sway and pat her on the back. I now remember the months I spent doing this. N looks up at me suspiciously. He looks even more boy-like as I look down at him while holding this other, tiny baby. I suddenly get a glimpse of what it might be like to have more than one child, to be holding one baby while the older one plays close by, watching. Life would feel very full up, even more than it does now. I realise I will want to have another baby before too long. I hand the baby back.

Packing

One of the many things that separates life with a baby from life without is the packing. When you go away for a weekend and you don't have a baby, you can fit everything you need for two people into one medium-sized holdall. When you go away for a weekend with a small baby, you can fit everything you need into one medium-sized car, and then only just. A baby needs a lot of stuff, or you *think* he needs a lot of stuff, which amounts to the same thing. The buggy takes up a great deal of room, or it does if you have bought an expensive, designer-type buggy like ours that lets your baby face you (when yours turns out to be a baby who doesn't want to face you), instead of a cheaper one that folds up into a stick. Then there are the bottles, the steriliser, the cartons of milk, the jars and jars of food, the baby rice cakes, the tiny boxes of raisins, the bananas for breakfast, the sticks of cheese and fruit for chewing in the car, the bowls and spoons to eat everything with. And then there is the travel cot, the sheets and blankets, the sleeping bag, the babygros for sleeping in, the short-sleeved vests for wearing underneath the other clothes, the trousers, long-sleeved tops, jumpers, cardigans, socks, coat, hat, shoes for wearing in the daytime. Even if you are going away for just two days, you assume you will need four of everything as you must be prepared for accidents, as they seem to happen whenever you aren't at home. Then there are the nappies, the nappy bags, the nappy cream, the thermometer for the bath, the play mat to sit on, the toys to throw around, the books to read, the plastic piano to play. Really it would be easier just to pick up the whole house with its baby paraphernalia and move it to wherever one is supposed to be going. Packing takes forever. When travelling with a baby, always aim to leave the house an hour earlier than you need to. You will still be late, but at least you will have given yourselves a chance.

igeons

N is six months old when he first notices the pigeons. We are sitting in Russell Square and I am giving him his milk. It is a sunny afternoon and once he's finished his bottle I lift him out of his buggy and stand him on my lap. Recently he has started to enjoy trying to bear his own weight on his legs, so I stand him on my knees and bounce him around for a bit, feeling guilty that he has spent too much time in his buggy this morning. He is peering down at a spot somewhere beyond his feet. I look down too and see the pigeon he is staring at; he is following its jerky running movement with his eyes as it scuttles around my boots. He cranes his neck over and beyond his feet, beyond my lap, to see the bird as it pecks and picks at things. As it disappears from view, under our bench, N looks up and out into the world again, searching for the next moving object to focus on, now that he has got the hang of it. His eyes fall on a jogger running along the gravel path in front of us. He turns his head to watch her properly as she races past us towards the gate at the end of the square. The pigeon, and now the jogger, are revelations to him. Suddenly, he is concentrating on all the moving creatures in the world. Until now, I've pushed him hopefully up to the edge of the lake in the park and pointed out the ducks, the swans, the black moorhens floating there in front us while he stares at something completely different, like the screw on the side of his buggy, or the underside of his sleeping bag. And now, today, here in this square, the change. There is a world of creatures out there and they move unpredictably, and go off and away. Another pigeon flutters down in front of us and starts scrabbling around on the path and N is all silent concentration again. We sit on the bench for a long time, with N watching the world go by. For the first time, I understand properly what this phrase means.

lastic

I vowed we'd never buy plastic toys. But here N sits, crashing out tunes on his plastic baby-walker-cum-piano with its dozen buttons. It is the noisiest, ugliest toy we could find in the shop, and N loves it. There is a Hawaiian-type tune that bursts out 'Dance to the island beat', followed by the sound of fake steel drums: it is one of the less excruciating riffs, which tells you all you need to know about this machine. It occasionally makes a 'Yee hah' noise, like someone giddying up a horse. And there are lots of lights that flash. N bangs away at it like a busy typist, engrossed, smiling and cooing at its crazy sounds. When he had a dose of the winter vomiting bug, it was this machine that kept him occupied between bouts of being sick. Now, beside me, he grabs and hits, mouth wide open in concentration, stretching out to reach the lit-up keys, reaching down to roll the plastic drums. Soon our house will be full of objects like this.

ℙ*oppers*

Once you have a baby, small fastenings – zips and buttons and poppers – assume a significance you never could have imagined before. Poppers fasten babygros together. Babies, on the whole, hate having babygros put on, and often scream and thrash about during the process. The aim is to be as fast as possible. The babygro I have just dressed N for bed in has an unnecessary number of poppers. For some reason, it has poppers all the way up one side, as well as on the inside of both legs (which is standard). It also has a single fiddly popper on the inside, to give it a chic, kimono look, and this hidden popper is extremely hard to find. It involves turning the dimmed-for-bedtime light back up again to full brightness in order for me to be able to locate it. It takes me three times as long to get N into this babygro as into any other item of clothing we own, and it feels like it takes years to get even an ordinary babygro on him at the end of the day. I must remember never to dress him in it again, because to do so is to enter a world of pain, confusion and prolonged screaming. Whoever designed it has never had a baby, of this I am certain. I feel I ought to write to him or her, explaining how complicated it is to dress a baby in this fashionable but totally impractical garment. Of course I will never actually do this.

Pregnancy

I am writing this when no longer pregnant. From this vantage point, pregnancy seems distant, alien, unreal. I can hardly remember what it was like. I am amnesiac about it, just as I am amnesiac about N as a younger baby, as any other baby than the one in front of me now.

I know that I spent the first three months of pregnancy feeling either very tired or very angry, and often both things at once. I was very happy to be pregnant, but I was still furious. I have a strong memory of screaming at D in a field full of cows one morning when I was about ten weeks in. We had gone for a walk and taken a wrong turn. We weren't very lost at all; we knew which way we needed to go next, which was back down through the field we'd just crossed. But even so I started yelling. I stamped my walking-boot-clad feet. I had to sit down on a tree trunk and take deep breaths. D couldn't understand what the fuss was about, and nor could I. My mood was doing something against my will. It was a sunny day and we were out in the hills and I was pregnant, but my mood was as dark as the clouds that usually hung over this bit of Wales. I went back to the house and slept for the rest of the day.

After the first twelve weeks, I got my energy back. I no longer spent every evening on the sofa. I felt so normal I started to wonder if I was still pregnant. I checked my stomach obsessively, looking for signs. I stood in profile in front of the mirror. I was relieved when I started to show because it meant something was still happening in there. Even though I didn't need them yet, I wanted to buy maternity clothes as a confirmation of my new state. I went to a maternity shop in my lunch break and browsed the racks. Perhaps if I had known then that I would be wearing them for many months, even after the birth, when nothing else would fit, I wouldn't have been so eager to buy these oversized garments. But I didn't know, so I bought myself a pair of jeans with a magic elasticated waistline.

During the middle part of my pregnancy, we spent our time doing the things everyone told us we should do. We saw friends, we went out. We went to the theatre and the cinema because we knew we would soon be going there a lot less. I was strangely calm. For the first time in years, I was able to get into lifts without fear. I was getting heavier, so stairs were harder, but I didn't feel anything like my usual anxiety about the possibility of the lift I was travelling in breaking down. I was as unneurotic as I've ever been: the pregnancy hormones were at work. I was so relaxed I hardly knew myself. I decided I would be much happier in life if I was always pregnant.

As the weeks went by, I read my pregnancy book obsessively. It was structured week-by-week. I felt superstitious about reading too many weeks ahead, so I tried to ration my reading to one section a week. The book would report: 'Week ten. Your baby now has ears, but can't hear anything.' I knew exactly what week I was at. Sometimes I would count off on my hands how many I had to go. Each new week of the pregnancy was marked in the book by a new stage of development. 'Your baby,' it would say, 'now weighs the same as half a bag of sugar.' I would find this new fact extraordinary, but hard to connect with. I needed the book to convince myself it was all still going on. There were other reminders: I had the photos from the two scans, which I kept hidden in my work diary. And of course I had those maternity jeans.

People divide pregnancy into thirds: the first, second and third trimester. My third trimester started around Christmas, about two weeks before D and I got married. We'd planned a small wedding, so my only real anxiety was about whether I'd still fit into the dress I'd bought in early

December. The wedding proved a great distraction from the fact that my pregnancy was coming to an end. After it there were no distractions left.

I was big and heavy now. The women I'd met on the NCT course who were at the same stage of pregnancy had stopped working. My plan was to keep going for as long as I could. It was part of my being in denial about actually having to give birth. If I was still going to the office, I couldn't be about to go into labour, could I? I lumbered onto packed commuter trains, telling myself I would keep going.

We spent a lot of time in department stores in those final weeks. I became very serious about shopping for baby equipment. We bought a Moses basket, babygros, sheets, muslins. I needed to know we had these things in the house. We piled them into the spare room in a big heap and closed the door on them.

The baby was kicking me a lot now, in the ribs and in the side. Sometimes I'd feel a foot or an elbow poking out of me, and I'd try and touch it before it disappeared back in, like a fast, wriggly fish. My stomach would ripple in waves, as the baby turned and kicked and tried to get comfortable. Sometimes I would feel the long hardness of a leg or arm. Other times I'd feel the solid roundness of a bum or a head – it was hard to tell which. He got hiccups a lot and I felt him jolting inside me. He was starting to feel heavy and solid, which meant I was starting to feel heavy and solid too. He was getting bigger and my stomach was squashed: it was hard to eat. I started to get Braxton Hicks contractions: my stomach went rock hard and tight, like a shell closing up.

They made it feel like I was suffocating inside and I had to sit very straight and upright in order to breathe. I was too big for some of my maternity clothes. My fingers swelled up until my new too-big wedding ring was suddenly too small, so I had to swap and wear D's. I was expanding, expanding, like Violet Beauregarde in *Charlie and the Chocolate Factory*. I was expanding so fast I worried I might explode.

By the end, I wanted the baby out. I was massive and my mind was foggy and I wanted pregnancy to be over. It got so that it was hard to sit up in bed from a lying position. It got so that it was uncomfortable to sit on the sofa and impossible to get off it. I was stuck, stranded; I was a beached whale. There was nothing left to do but have this baby. I finally stopped working and started waiting.

Questioning

His first birthday is approaching, and everything in life is a question for N. He asks questions by holding something – a book, a block – then looking up at me, before handing the object towards me. As he holds whatever it is he has up for inspection, he makes an ascending sound with his voice, a bit like the brrrm, brrrm noise he makes for a bus, a sort of rising '*errrrrhhhhhhhh*?' sound. It is the sound of a question. I hadn't noticed until N started asking them that a question has an identifiable sound. N looks puzzled as he makes this noise and stares up at me. This is his way of asking: 'What is this?' Or: 'What is happening here?' And so I tell him. I tell him Farmer Fred is in his shed and working really hard. I tell him it's a round/square/long block he's holding up for me to see. I tell him it's blue or pink or orange or a triangle. He is looking for certainty each time; he needs every question to have an answer.

uiet

The quiet of the house when N has just gone to sleep is a very quiet sort of quiet. We are trying not to wake him, because when he rests, we and the whole house rest.

eal world

I realise this morning that we have not opened our post for two months now. It has been piling up like snowdrifts on our hall table. We have been good about many household things, but it seems to be the post we can't cope with. I force myself to sit down and go through it, grimly. I open the over-the-overdraft-limit bank statements from last month – my last month of unpaid maternity leave when, not surprisingly, we had, finally, completely run out of money. I open the electricity bill; the mobile phone bill; the traffic fine for being caught on camera waiting in a yellow box back when N was only two months old and I was probably too tired even to have noticed the markings on the road.

The post is the real world, of course, and it is this I'm avoiding. People warn you about the responsibilities of parenthood, but now that we have N, I feel more in denial about the real world than ever. When I go out into it, it is for brief and specific forays: to the office for nine hours; to the shops for milk. I am not in the world in the way I used to be. I dip my toe into it briefly, and then I always retreat, promptly, towards home.

ed hair

N's father has black hair. I have brown hair. N's is vivid red. We discover from my uncle that there is a hidden branch of my father's family known as the 'Ginger Birnes'. The things that you cannot get away from. It is lovely on N, though.

Rocking

When he cries or when he is tired, the best way to comfort N is to stand and hold him and rock him. I hold his head under my chin and I sway from one side to the other, from one hip back onto the other. I am like a boat going up and down and N is my small passenger. I find myself rocking even when I am not holding N. In the evening, when he is asleep in his cot, I will stand at the stove cooking rice, or stand in the kitchen holding a glass of wine, rocking from one side to the other, swaying like a tree. I catch myself doing it and laugh at myself, and try to stop, but then I'll fall back into it again. Once you have a baby, your body learns rhythms and movements that belong to that baby, so that even when your baby is elsewhere – asleep upstairs, or being looked after by someone else – you find yourself settling into the very same patterns. At a drinks party in a grand room in a hotel, my first semi-work event since having N, I am standing in the middle of a crowd, wearing my black dress, clutching a glass of champagne, trying not to rock and sway, rock and sway. I am trying to stand still like all the other people here. I am trying to talk about grown-up things, not baby things, and I am trying to stay in one place as I do it. I feel the swaying and rocking will give me away.

Routine

Every evening after I have taken N's nappy off and let him kick around and then given him his bath and taken him out of the bath and brought him back into his bedroom and wound up his favourite Fisher Price clock (the Fisher Price clock I had as a baby), and smeared nappy cream and baby balm on his skin and put a clean nappy on him and dressed him in a clean babygro and zipped him into his sleeping bag and fed him his bottle of milk and laid him down in his cot asleep, I stand at the kitchen sink, washing up the bottles from the day. N is five months old now, and we have had this bedtime routine going for the past two months. The scary baby books are very big on the idea of a bedtime routine and it is the one thing they recommend that we have persisted with. I have been washing bottles at this time every evening for the past two months, and as I stand and wash them, I think about the fact that at this time tomorrow evening I will be here at this same sink washing these same bottles. And again the evening after that. Every now and then I am panicked by this thought. Then I go online and search for theatre tickets or cinema listings. I decide that we will have to leave N with his grandmother for an evening as soon as possible so that we can break up the inevitability of this bottle-washing. But then I forget to book the tickets or decide I can't quite be bothered to go into town. Breaking the routine, going out, would take a mammoth effort. Staying home, sticking with the routine, is easier. It is the bottle-washing that sometimes gets to me. There are so many bottles.

owing

D is forty minutes late home from work this evening, as he is most evenings. Some evenings he is much, much later than this, but on a normal day forty minutes is as good as it gets in terms of not really being that late at all. But for some reason, today I can't handle this lateness. I am furious about it. It has been a dull, indoorsy, winter's day, and I have been trying to send some emails and N has been a bit toothy and grizzly and I am annoyed at having got nothing done. I tell myself I can do the things I need to do when D gets home to put N in the bath. Bath time arrives and there is no D, so I take N up myself and bath him and dress him to much screaming, and then I give him his milk and try and settle him in his cot. He will not settle because of his teeth so I carry him about a bit and then I put him down again and I wind his clock up and I leave him to it. I can hear him muttering on the baby monitor as I clear up the kitchen. D arrives and comes down to say hello. He is very happy to be home, but I am stony silent, and then I pick up an oven tray from the drying rack and fling it onto the floor by his feet. It makes a rattly, tinny noise that sounds good. Then I start shouting. I am furious that he is always late. On my days in the office, I leave work on time, I say. I don't have the luxury of staying late. I have to get home to relieve H. Why can't he do the same? I accuse him of thinking my job is less important than his now that I work four days not five and am earning less money than he is. I scream and leave the kitchen. Until I started shouting, I hadn't realised I felt this strongly about it. When D comes to find me, he is apologetic. He says he will try to leave work earlier in future. I know we will row about this again.

$\boxed{S}$can *(14 weeks)*

At the fourteen-week scan I stared down at my shoes as the ultrasound woman got her wand ready and smothered my stomach with gel. I had on my character shoes (with heels). I had worn them specially; I think I was resisting becoming mumsy too soon. Lying on the bed, I stared down at these colourful shoes, which looked suddenly strange on my feet, and when I looked up from them, there on the screen beside me was my baby. Well, she or he was becoming a baby. It was tiny and at the same time perfectly clear and detailed. I was stunned. The ultrasound woman ran her wand round and over my stomach and showed us the different parts: the legs, the arms, the stomach. I found myself marvelling at the fact that those things were there already. I think D may have been a bit tearful. We went for a sandwich straight afterwards and D put his head down on the table in the café because he was suddenly exhausted – as though he was having a premonition of the sleepless nights to come. We had bought a photo of the scan and I put it in my diary. It was black and fuzzy but you could still make out the shape, reclining there in the dark. For weeks afterwards I would sneak it out and look at it, often two or three times a day. It felt like our secret, proof that she or he really was here.

Scan (20 weeks)

We had decided to find out the sex of this baby at the twenty-week scan. We both felt sure we were going to have a girl. 'What would you like?' the ultrasound man asked us, rather unkindly, as his wand hovered over my now quite large stomach. He was speaking as though the matter had yet to be decided and the final choice ultimately rested with him and his magic wand. 'We don't mind,' I replied firmly, before D could say anything, 'so long as he or she is healthy.' 'Well, it's a boy,' he said, pointing out the boyish bits on the scan, and I couldn't believe it, I had been so totally certain it was a girl in there. 'A boy?' 'A boy!' I kept saying, as though that would help it sink in.

That evening we went to visit my parents. They picked us up from the station. We were both quiet in the back of the car, still trying to take this boyness in. My parents were desperate to ask, I could tell, but didn't dare, so I told them as casually as I could. 'So we're having a boy.' They took us to a nearby pub and we chose a table by the fireplace. At some point during his first pint, D reached out to a stack of second-hand books that were piled up for sale in the fireplace.

He pulled the top book idly off the pile and looked at it. He stared at it. Then he held it up to me, showing me the cover: *Boy*, it said, by Roald Dahl. (We bought it.) Even if we hadn't had the scan, we'd have known from that point on.

itting

I am not sure exactly how old N was when he learnt to sit up on his own. But here he sits in front of me, upright, playing with his treasure basket, going through it methodically, pulling out one object and turning it over, then throwing it aside and pulling out another. His lower lip juts out in concentration. His eyes are cast down, fixed on the silver medal he has pulled out and is now turning over and over in his hands, watching as it shines under the bright lights. Was it at six months he learnt to sit up? Or seven? It was probably somewhere in between. But it has happened so gradually, his really being able to do it, that I am suddenly struck by the fact that a few weeks ago I had a helpless baby, flat on his back, and here now I somehow have a sitting-up-unsupported one. The sitting means he can explore the world more effectively – he can reach out for things and grab them, mainly things in this basket, which he never seems to get bored of. He can stretch a long way forward, much further than I ever would have thought, without toppling over onto his head. He stretches to grab a plastic cup or the bag of Christmas tree bells, and then he pulls himself upright again, object in hand, raising it up to his face to get a good look. Then after a while he drops it, looks about him on the mat for something else, reaches off, down to the left now, retrieves his wooden maraca, and sits there proudly waving it in the air. With this sitting and this reaching for objects he has become a baby with interests and inclinations. He always takes the wooden mop out of the treasure basket first, for instance. He is never much interested in the smooth, wooden pebble, which I'd been sure he would enjoy turning over and over. The sitting makes him more self-sufficient for periods of time than I would ever have imagined an eight-month-old baby could be. Watching him as he gets more confident at it, I understand the point of sitting all over again. It is so we can rest and occupy ourselves and get things done: typing, reading, rummaging through treasure baskets.

ize

My friend J has lent me some red suede baby shoes. They are sitting on the hall table. They are too big for N, who is five months old and who has recently seemed so robust, but still they look almost unbearably tiny sitting there in the hall. I should put them back in the bag, pack them away until N's feet are big enough for them, but I love the reminder of their tininess. He won't be this small for ever.

Sleeping

I lay N in his cot when it's about the right time for his nap and when he starts to rub his eyes or yank at his ears. Then I watch for a bit to check I've got the timing right. A sign that I haven't got the timing right is when N starts thrashing about on the mattress, laughing and giggling. But if he stretches himself out gratefully and starts to stare out at some object – the mobile hanging off the paper lampshade in front of his cot, for example – then I know he's in the right place. I know he is getting ready to go off when he puts one hand on top of the other on top of his chest and holds them, a bit like a praying mantis. He turns his head to stare at the light coming in through the gap in the wooden shutters. Then he turns his head back towards me to check I'm still here, sitting on the sofa next to his cot. Then he turns back to stare at the gap in the shutters some more. Then back to me. Then back to the shutters. Now he closes his eyes. He opens them again. He closes them. Opens. Closes. They stay closed. He is gone, he is asleep. I tiptoe out of the room and leave him to it.

Silence in the house. Time to do all the things I can't do when he is awake.

Creeping back up to N's cot about ten minutes later, he is deep in it, dreaming of who knows what. Milk? The swings? The cat at M's house? His dummy moves up and down, and his chest slowly rises and falls, but other than that, he is still and heavy. A baby's sleep is faraway and mysterious. It is private, like the sleep life of adults.

When N is properly, deeply asleep, he sleeps with his two fists up at either side of his head, like a boxer in deep repose. He has slept like this since we stopped swaddling him. He has always wanted to sleep like this, which was why we stopped swaddling him. We have photos of him in his Moses basket at a few weeks old with his arms up in this strong-man pose. Right now, lying like this, he seems very close to being a newborn again. I like to be reassured of this, of his proximity to being a tiny baby. I don't want these baby months to fly by too fast.

N sleeps on and I go back downstairs and scuttle round the house sorting things out like a wind-up doll. I put another load of washing on. I fold clean clothes away. I half-empty the dishwasher. And suddenly, in the middle of all this, a scream. Lights flash all over the baby monitor. N is awake and yelling. He is shocked at having fallen asleep in the middle of the day like this, even though he does it every day. He is confused. He wants to come out. NOW. The screams get louder and louder as I frantically climb the stairs to save him. When I appear at the door of his room, saying, 'It's all right, it's all right,' the screaming stops and he is all smiles and beams. I scoop him up out of his cot and he pushes back from me to look around him. He needs to look round the room again, urgently. He needs to remind himself about this place, this world that he left for half an hour back there.

Sleeplessness

Just before his first Christmas, N catches a cold and nights are agony. He will not sleep, he cannot sleep. He can't even lie down in his cot. He needs to sit up. He needs to be with one of us all the time. He screams and screams if he doesn't have the right thing to distract him. The right thing turns out to be a psychedelic TV programme called *In the Night Garden*. D and I take it in turns each night to stay up with him. At four in the morning, with no sleep between us so far, N and I sit next to the lit-up Christmas tree, watching Iggle Piggle dancing with his blanket; the Tombliboos putting their trousers on, playing with their ball. I am queasy with tiredness. It feels as if I have been at an all-night party, but with none of the fun. I try not to look at the clock any more, it makes me feel too ill. After a while, *In the Night Garden* has calmed him down enough so that I can sit him in his buggy, here in the living room, and he doesn't cry to find himself there. I lie next to him on the sofa. After a while, I drift off. I wake at some point and he is still upright in his buggy next to me, and somehow, miraculously, he has drifted off too.

Smiles

Like all babies' first smiles, N's are caused by wind. But then, slowly, his smiles change and start to seem deliberate. I have a photo of one of N's first real smiles. He is turning his head and smiling at D, who is sitting up in bed in his glasses. N has always loved D's glasses. If you look closely at the photo you can see that N is not in fact smiling at D, he is smiling at his glasses.

now

It is snowing. I watch it come down through the window. I bundle N up in his suddenly appropriately named snowsuit and put him in the buggy inside his sleeping bag and we go out into it. The snow is falling in big white chunks. It is proper snow, Disney snow. I put the rain cover over the buggy as it is snowing quite hard, but I leave the lid open near N's face so he can see out. I want him to see this, his first snow. I am excited for him as he silently watches the flakes, interested in it the way he is interested in rain or leaves or ducks on the pond. The snow settles on the rain cover and sits there in clumps before melting. N bats his hand at it just as he bats at the soap bubbles I blow for him. As we walk through the park, past the freezing ducks on the frozen lake, I try to watch the snow for the first time too. It is very bright. The flakes are huge and coming at us diagonally. I want it to settle so N can see what it looks like as a carpet. I want him to blink at the whiteness of the place. I am always happy when it snows, but this year I am happier than usual because it is snowing for him.

We get a lot of snow this winter. It snows particularly hard one week, and on the third morning of snow I realise that N has not left the house for more than two days. (He has been at home with H, who is sensible about these things; I have been working in town, where the pavements are mostly walkable.) I decide he needs fresh air, now, and so I invent an excuse to go out (going out of the house with a baby is often on some invented premise, even on the non-snowiest of days) and the excuse is sausages. I decide we must have them for dinner this evening, and not just any old sausages: the good ones from the butcher's a ten-minute walk away. I get N into his layers and then into his buggy. At the open front door I pause at the top of the steps and survey the street. The pavements are grey with sludge and ice. The cars are white. So is the road. I take off my furry boots and put my wellies on instead and, because I can see that special measures are required, wrap the strap which attaches to the buggy round my wrist in case I fall over and the buggy should carry on by itself on the ice. Once down our ice-free front steps (there is a boiler down below), I slither down the pavement and along the street.

I soon discover how difficult it is trying to push a buggy in the snow and ice. I discover that, while I may want to walk one way, in a straight line, the buggy seems determined to veer off to the right. I am constantly trying to correct it, while staying upright in my wellies. We move along at a snail's pace. I lean over to check how N is coping and he seems to be finding it all quite amusing. And, even better, so far his mittens, which for once I remembered, are still on him. We make our creeping way under the viaduct and across the (gritted!) pedestrian crossing and head, optimistically, in the direction of the butcher's and then the park. On the next street, I discover the dangers of the handy slopes they have created on pavements to help blind people and people with buggies and wheelchairs to cross roads. The slopes are like mini ski-runs in the ice. At the third slope, indeed, I become a skier and find myself sliding towards the road, two green boots moving ahead of me as I flail around. I grab onto a luckily located pole and spin into it. The buggy, thankfully, slithers to a stop with me. I collect myself and take hold of the buggy handle again. I really ought to be sensible and abort this mission. We forget all about the butcher's with its superior sausages that is still several ice-lined streets away and settle for the supermarket, which is just round the corner. I buy milk, bread and lots and lots of baby food. I want to buy water, batteries, multiple tins of beans, as I feel we should be stockpiling in this kind of weather, but I have no way of carrying it all. We slither home, the shopping bag under the buggy full to bursting, threatening to spill its load of jars of baby food into the road at every slippery turn.

ocks

N does not like wearing socks. They never stay on his feet for long, unless they are protected by boots that are laced on tight. I put the socks on him and within three minutes they are ripped off, thrown aside. His feet are always cold. I put the socks back on him three, four times a day. He takes them off as fast as he can. Someone suggests he should wear tights, but I suspect that would make him very angry. He also likes to take the socks off babies he is playing with. I think their mothers find this less amusing than I do.

Stalling

I am stalling right now. N should be at A's house, with H, the nanny. But instead he is upstairs napping in his own cot. Partly, this is because I am afraid of him sleeping at A's house: they have a cat, and I am scared of what she might do. (I know I am being mad, but I can't help it.) The other reason he is still here is that I don't want to have to be without him for any longer than I need to. He is supposed to be settling in with H: I go back to work next week. But this morning I decided not to let him go. We went for a long walk in the park instead, and then to baby music class. When we got home N had his milk and didn't eat his apple, pea and parsnip mush. And now he is having a nap. This was a stolen morning. I want to steal him again this afternoon, but I know I must take him to A's when he wakes up. He needs to get used to this new regime. I need to get used to it too. It feels wrong to be letting him go. I am not sure I want to get used to it.

Talking

When I pick N up and say, 'Hello,' sometimes he makes a noise that is like '*Allo*'. He has made this noise since he was about four months old (I think). When he is excited he goes, '*Ooaah, ooaahh, ooaahh,*' and sometimes kicks his legs at the same time. His friend M goes, '*Yeah, yeah, yeah, yeah, yeah,*' and N sits opposite and laughs and laughs at him. Sometimes, in the middle of the night, if his teeth are bothering him, he'll put his fingers on his lower jaw and babble, '*Agggh, agggh, agggh, agggh, agggh.*' All his words have a rhythm. '*Aaaagggh aaaaggghhhhhaaa,*' he'll moan when he's not happy about something, or if something is out of reach, or he's frustrated. '*Gahhhh, oooaaah, oooooaahhh,*' he'll say when he finally gets hold of it, a maraca for instance, and waves it in front of his face, proudly.

And then, when he is eleven months and one day, he starts talking in a different way. '*Bah, bah, bah, bah, bah, bah,*' he says over and over. '*Bah, bah, bah, bah, bah.*' The bahs come out of him in a long string of sounds. I can tell this is his version of talking in complete sentences. '*Bah, bah, bah, bah, bah, bah, bah, bah,*' is N having a conversation with himself. He says it all the way home on the bus and then all the way down the street and across the park. He talks to himself in his cot way, way into the evening, way past his normal bedtime. '*Bah, bah, bah, bah, bah,*' goes the baby monitor. '*Bah, bah, bah, bah, bah, bah.*' Now that he can talk, he doesn't need to sleep. I wonder what it is he thinks he is saying. I think it is nice that his first words aren't 'Da' or 'Ma' but something in between. As he gets older, when he talks to himself, it sounds like he is speaking Japanese.

antrums

Everyone knows toddlers have tantrums, but babies have them too. In our house, these sometimes happen at breakfast time. N likes a concoction called Baby Brekkie in the mornings. It is made of yoghurt and rice and bananas and he laughs when he sees the packet coming his way and opens his mouth extra wide for the spoon. His liking it so much is all very cute, but it often goes wrong when the packet is finished and I have to get up and throw it away. I stand up with the empty packet and N screws up his face. His mouth turns down into his grumpy boy face. He looks like a gargoyle when he does this, but he is not as still. His eyes fill with tears. He starts screaming and his face turns bright red. I try to give him toast to help him forget about the Baby

Brekkie, and sometimes this works. On other mornings, though, all toast is refused and the screaming goes on and on until the only thing for it is to give him another sachet. He is eleven months old and he knows exactly what he wants.

D leaves his laptop on the floor. N scoots over to it, starts hitting the keys, poking the screen. I scoop him up, tell him no, carry him away from it. The mouth turns down, the eyes water, the screaming starts. He goes rigid and his back arches. He is furious with me. He will not even look at me. I have thwarted him.

eeth

At ten months and three weeks, N has his first tooth. I catch sight of it poking through the middle of his bottom gum when I am spooning mashed-up fish pie into his mouth. He has grown this tooth overnight. He woke at three a.m. and I brought him into our bed, where he fell asleep. He woke again a few hours later, cross with whatever it was that had woken him up (the tooth, I suppose). We gave him Calpol, the magic pink stuff. He went back to sleep. He woke at eight a.m. With a tooth. I feel ridiculously proud of him.

elevision

You no longer need television once you have a baby. This is because you have a baby to watch instead. D and I spend hours each day just watching N. When you are tired and amazed there is sometimes nothing else you can do.

hree months

'When does it get easier?' is the question mothers of new-borns seem to ask other mothers most often. 'At three months,' seems to be the standard reply. N is three and a half months and he has just started to sleep through the night. He can go until six a.m. for a feed now, as long as we give him a bottle at eleven p.m. I still wake in the night expecting him to wake too, but this is hardly his fault. Three months may really be the magic number. Whether it is or not, I start to tell other mothers with brand new babies that it is; it gives them a sense of an end of sorts in sight.

ime

Before we had N we must have had a lot of time on our hands. We must have had so much spare time that we didn't know what to do with it. We spend hours each day looking after him now: getting him dressed; feeding him breakfast; feeding him lunch; feeding him dinner; giving him his bottles; playing with him; singing to him; holding him; reading to him; pushing him to the park in his buggy; playing with him some more; settling him in his cot for his naps and running up and down the stairs to him when this is going wrong; bathing him; getting him ready for bed; settling him in bed for the night and then rocking him back to sleep when he wakes up. Then there are all the other things we need to do that are connected to him: washing his clothes and hanging them up to dry; folding them up and putting them away; making his food; wiping the table, the high chair after he's had his food; cleaning his bottles; stocking up his nappy bag and the nappy baskets under his changing table; emptying the nappy bin; tidying up his toys; tidying them up a second time after he has taken them all out again. Buying the milk, the food, the nappies, the wipes, and trying to make sure we don't run out of any of them. Ever. Sometimes, I wonder how we spent each weekday evening before we had N, before one of us (me) had to rush home for bath, milk, bed.

I don't have much time for myself these days (this is such an obvious statement, there seems little point in writing it down). Time not at work is time spent passing a squeaky rubber giraffe from hand to hand because that is what N wants to do. It is time spent reading books where a mouse is the main character over and over again. Time for myself is in the two- or three-hour slot after N has gone to bed (if he has gone to bed) and before I finally give in and go to bed too. Eventually I realise that some aspects of going to work – the journey there, the detour to buy a coffee to take to my desk, the lunch breaks when I have not arranged a meeting – are a kind of free time: in these moments I have only myself to organise and to please. There is no point resenting the loss of time for myself – this is what having a baby means – but sometimes the extent of it shocks me.

oys

N starts to accumulate toys slowly, and then, at Christmas, very quickly. We write a list of the toys he is given so we can write thank-you cards. The list is as follows:

A red wooden bus with wooden people inside (from us). The label claims the bus is suitable from ten months, but N is nine months, and the only part of it he seems to understand after we've opened the box and set it up for him are the two wooden planks with round holes bored into them: these are meant to be the platforms on which the wooden peg people sit. He turns the planks over and over, pushes his fingers into the holes. The bus and the people mean nothing to him yet, but the holes in the planks are amazing.

A metal spinning top, a red plastic car that revs up and has pop-up headlights, a fabric 'My First Toolbox' toolbox filled with a squidgy fabric hammer, spanner, pliers and screwdriver (all these things from my parents). N likes to watch the spinning top as it goes round on the floor. He keeps staring at it: he is in a spinning-top-induced trance. He laughs and tries to grab it, and when he grabs it, it naturally stops. He is very interested in the contents of the toolbox, especially the screwdriver. It is long and pointy and rattles and he likes passing it from hand to hand. He also likes the fabric toolbox itself. It has a zip, and he is obsessed with zips, specifically with touching the tag that opens and shuts the zip. He also likes turning the empty toolbox upside down and putting it on his head. He is a little scared of the plastic car and I think he is right to be.

A wooden 'activity cube' (from D's mother). This is a giant wooden cube with a clock on one side, a xylophone on another, a blackboard on another, and a set of spinning wooden letters arranged as an alphabet on the last side. On the top panel there are beads threaded on metal wires that criss-cross over each other like a spaghetti junction. N likes the beads on the wires, trying to rattle them, but not as much as he likes trying to push the cube over, or pull it on top of himself, and I have to hold it down to stop him: it is sharp and heavy. I put the cube away under a side table, trying to hide it. It is quite big and makes the room look smaller than it used to.

A trolley of wooden blocks (from D's father). N is suspicious of these blocks. He will not touch them, apart from the two green cone-shaped ones with round blue beads on top, which look alarmingly like wooden breasts. Very occasionally, he will dare to pick up the pink one with the wooden ball that makes a rattling sound and the blue one with the bell in it. But the other forty-odd blocks in the trolley he will not touch. He will, however, touch the wheels of the trolley itself. He likes to stroke them. Another toy he will grow into, I tell myself, as I shove it discreetly under the sofa.

A giraffe bath toy (from D's sister). It has suckers so you can stick it onto the side of the bath tub. My father nearly comes a cropper on Boxing Day morning when he steps into the tub for a shower and slips on the giraffe and a few of her turtle friends.

A wind-up plastic swimming whale (from my grandmother). It comes with a miniature yellow baby whale that spurts water from the top of its head. This makes N laugh.

A crinkly book called *Fishy Tails* (from my sister). This is the companion volume to N's second favourite crinkly book, *Jungly Tails*. He appreciates the fishy version – in particular, the long green plastic tail that sticks out of one of the pages – but he prefers the jungly original. He is loyal in this way.

I am not sure what one baby is supposed to do with so many toys. He isn't at all sure either. Mostly, he plays with those he already knows. It is those I spend most time tidying up at the end of each day.

Trains

Coming home from my first day back at work, the train doors close but the train remains stationary on the platform. After a couple of minutes a sense of panic starts to rise up in me. 'Get moving,' a voice in my head is shouting, 'get me back to N. NOW.' But the train remains stuck on the platform. My heart starts to beat faster in my chest. The palms of my hands feel damp. I wonder if this is what the start of a panic attack feels like. I undo my coat and want to know how hard it would be to open a window. When finally the train creaks and shudders and pulls slowly away, I feel intense relief. I am going back to him. I will the train to go faster, faster, to get me home.

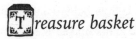reasure basket

N's treasure basket is a round wicker tray filled with household objects. Its contents include a plastic egg cup; a yellow tin of mustard powder (sealed); a black ribbon; a kitchen spoon; a rubber ball; a carpet square; a pastry cutter; a bag of Christmas bells; a wooden pebble; a napkin ring; a small blue maraca; a pack of playing cards. When he is eight months old, he sits in front of the basket for half an hour at a time, pulling one thing out, turning it over in his hand, or shaking it, or passing it from one hand to another. After a while, he throws whatever it is he has been holding onto the floor and pulls out another object. He goes through it like an old man going through his underwear drawer: busily, and with total concentration.

Trial run

The hardest day was the trial run. I took N to A's house and left him there with M and H. I walked home with arms full of shopping bags and no N, and when I got home I put the bags on the floor in the hall and I wailed. My whole body was convulsing. I think I was tearing at my hair. I know I was shouting at myself. I know I shouted at D when he phoned up. I shouted about how stupid I was to be letting this happen when N was still only eight months old. It didn't matter to me then that we had run out of money, that we couldn't pay the mortgage, that I had to go back to work. I had let N down, I had separated us too soon. I had broken something and it would never be fixed. I cried most of the afternoon without him. I knew I was making a terrible mistake, but that there was nothing I could do about it. I felt as though the damage had been done. When I think about that afternoon now, when I write about it, I shiver. When N got home that night after his first afternoon with H, he refused to look at me. I cried more quietly after he went to bed.

Trying to have a baby

You can't be sure if it is going to work until it happens, and you have no way of knowing when that will be. The uncertainty is overwhelming. You have spent much of your life not wanting to have a baby, and then a little time wondering whether in fact you might want to have a baby, until now, suddenly, you find yourself knowing in your bones that you *need* to have a baby. Now that you know it but can't magically make it happen, you live from month to month.

Trying to have it all

I have lunch with a woman I know who is in her late forties and who is therefore one generation of working mothers ahead of me. She is keen to hear how it is going for me back in the office. These are the early days and I tell her that I am struggling with it, struggling to leave N. She looks sympathetic, but I can tell from her face that she thinks I have it easy. As we eat, she tells me that she was given a promotion just before her first child was born. She worked in a design company and there was no chance of the job being left open for her to take maternity leave, so she didn't. She went back to work, to her new job, when her baby was just weeks old, because she had no choice. She sometimes took the baby into the office and left him in a Moses basket behind the door. She did the same thing with her second baby. When her youngest son was ten she took a career break between jobs. She says this was her version of maternity leave. But I think I notice tears in her eyes while she is speaking.

A little later I have tea with another woman in her forties with children: she has a big job in a distribution company. I am still finding work hard and I want to talk to someone who has returned and made a go of it. I emailed her in a panic from the office because it was a bad morning, and she rushed over to meet me in a café in my lunch hour. She came so fast and with so little fuss that I am sure she must know first-hand about panics like these.

She says she did manage to take maternity leave, but she

also took her babies into the office many times while on leave. When she went back to work after six months she worked full-time and long, hard hours, and did a lot of travelling. She does not sound happy when she talks about it. She tells me she missed out on too much. She says that if she could do things again, she would do them differently; she would spend more time with her babies. I sense real regret and I am frightened for myself in case I should ever feel it too. I had asked her to meet me because I had assumed she would talk me down, convince me of the importance of getting back to the office. But she seems to be telling me the opposite. I go back to work after our tea. I am more confused rather than less, but I am still, for the time being, back at my desk.

Both these women say they felt they had to show they could raise children but also get the biggest jobs and the biggest promotions. I am slightly shaken by their regrets. I want to work, but not at the expense of everything else (and I need the work to be interesting). Perhaps I am betraying the cause. I think, though, that the cause has probably betrayed itself already.

urning

At ten months, N still can't crawl and he can't leave the spot he is sitting on. He has, however, learned to rotate. He sits on his bottom and drags himself round, ninety, one-eighty, three hundred and sixty degrees. I leave him facing his toys and walk into the kitchen, and when I turn round he is facing the stove and no toys at all.

Twinkle, Twinkle, Little Star

I take N to a new mother-and-baby class at our local children's centre when he is two months old. They spend an hour telling us that it is good for our babies to spend time on their tummies. At the end of the class the midwife asks us to sit in a circle with our babies on our knees. Most of the babies are asleep or feeding. N is awake. The midwife starts to sing 'Twinkle, Twinkle, Little Star' and opens and closes her hands in the air, miming shining stars. N looks at her hands opening and closing. He watches her mouth as it sings. He smiles.

I sing the song to him when we get home and he smiles at me, too. Soon, I sing it all the time. I sing it when I am getting him dressed for bed and he is angry and wanting his milk. He stops crying and smiles and giggles; he can't help himself. I sing it to him when he is having his nappy changed and not in the mood for it. I sing it to him when I am strapping him into his buggy and he is getting mad with the straps. He never seems to get bored with the tune. Until one day, when he has just turned ten months old, I sing it and he starts to cry.

Underwear (or underwired)

Having a baby calls for new underwear, and not exciting, spoil-yourself underwear. First comes the pregnancy bra, which seems very flimsy and not up to the task. Then comes the nursing bra, which has clips that allow it to open up for feeding. After the breast-feeding is over, there is a period of time when you go on wearing the by now very manky maternity bras because your old bras don't fit and you can't face buying new, massive ones that won't be temporary but will be here to stay. In the end, after months of wearing horrible grey bras, I decide to get measured at a proper place. The two fitters are very polite and I leave the shop quite a lot poorer. These new items are not sexy, they are sturdy. They seem appropriate.

Unsolicited advice

People (women, mostly) find it impossible not to give the mothers of small babies advice. I am very bad at taking any kind of advice or instruction, so I find this situation very annoying. I have received lots of advice on the subject of N, most of it useless. The Polish woman on the No.55 bus pointed at N's bare feet and said: 'In Poland, our babies wear socks.' I could have drawn her attention to the fact that it was the middle of summer. I could have told her that the few times I *had* put socks on him, he had pulled them straight off and we'd lost them. But I didn't; I just smiled, because it seemed the easiest thing to do. Later, a woman on a busy street stopped me as I was pushing N in his buggy, fast, trying to get him out of the blazing sun and onto the shady bit of pavement, to tell me: 'Your baby is in the sun. You need to get him into the shade.' Often, when it comes to babies, advice is just a way of stating the utterly obvious.

There comes a time with some of the local mothers I know, as they are trying to stop breast-feeding and get their babies onto bottles, when I become the bottle-feeding agony aunt. This is not a role I have asked for. I resent being forced to give my opinion on particular teats, or different shapes of bottle. I tell them I gave N a bottle under strict instruction, he drank it, and that was it, but they seem unsatisfied by this explanation. I become increasingly annoyed by their desire to mark me out as a different species of mother with my bottle-feeding expertise.

When N is almost a year old I catch myself doling out unasked-for advice on the perplexing issue of naps to a friend with a much younger baby. I take myself quickly home and give myself a stern talking to.

accinations

Taking N for his vaccinations is torture – for him, for me. The doctor is fast and ruthless. He plunges a needle into N's right thigh – *jab*. N turns down his mouth and screams. There is no time for recovery; the doctor plunges a second needle into N's left thigh – *jab*. N screams some more. N is purple-blue with the screaming, and sort of choking as well. 'All done,' the doctor says cheerfully, shooing us out of the room, leaving me to wrestle a half-dressed, rigid, hysterical N, various clothes that need to go back on him, the buggy and the nappy bag out into the waiting room. The room is packed and all heads lift, all eyes focus on us as we emerge, still screaming.

Velcro

For a long time, N hates the sound of ripping Velcro, like the Velcro that fastens his bibs together; it makes him scream.

ater

N loves water. He loves his bath and he loves putting his
hands wherever water is: in cups and glasses and bowls. At
six months, I decide to take him to baby swimming classes.
I buy him a tiny wetsuit on eBay. We go along to our first
lesson with big expectations; I have heard about the magical
moment when a baby learns he can swim underwater. We
go into the changing rooms. There are babies lying on every
surface – crying babies, laughing babies, indifferent babies.
I find the only bit of surface that is left, a patch of marble
counter next to the sinks. I balance N on the small slab,
with his legs in the sink, and extract the eBay wetsuit from
my bag. The room is hot and noisy and we are right next to
the hand-dryer, as I discover when another mother turns it
on and N starts screaming. I start to undress N while shooting looks at the hand-drying mother and he is wriggly and
cross. I undo the Velcro fastenings on the wetsuit and he
screams more loudly. I get him into the suit and do up the

fastenings and N is still cross and cry-y. I have to put my
own costume on now. I leave N balanced precariously next
to the sink and get undressed, stopping to put a quick hand
on him whenever I think he might fall. I kick my trousers
off onto the floor and take out my new, enormous, mumsy
swimming costume. I wriggle myself into it and take out a
towel for N and a towel for me. Then I shove our clothes
back into the bag and pick up both bag and N and go over
to the lockers, which, it turns out, need a key, a thing I do
not have, so I shove the bag into an empty locker and shut
the door and hope that no one steals our clothes while we
are gone. Then I carry N through to the swimming pool.
The class before ours is just ending, and the pool is full of
mothers and their babies. The babies are swimming angeli-
cally on their mothers' chests, while the mothers swim on
their backs; other babies hold onto their mothers' necks
while the mothers swim on their fronts. The babies look
like little seals. They are happy and at home in the water,
swimming like I never could have imagined babies could,
and I start to think the palaver in the changing room may
have been worth it. After a few minutes, the class climbs
out, and it is our turn to climb in. I wade in, holding N to
my chest. The water is at knee height, then waist height,
and then N's toes are in the water, then his foot and the
bottom half of his leg. I am still holding him tight to me, but
as the water starts to reach his knees he howls. I smile at
him and start talking nonsense and carry on wading in, but
as the water rises higher and covers more of him, he howls
louder. I lift him up out of the water and hold him close to

my face and jiggle him about a bit and he calms down. This is good. After about a minute I lower him slowly back in, still holding him against me. As the water rises up over his legs he starts crying again.

The swimming teacher, a man in a waterlogged T-shirt, wants us all to gather in a circle, but N is crying hard and I am worried about him setting off the other babies. We must come into the circle, though, so we do, and N cries his way through the welcome song. Then the teacher tells us it is time to dunk our babies underwater. He tells us it is good to get this over with, but N is still crying. The teacher must see the look on my face because he tells me we can sit this one out just this week. I hold N against me and watch as the other mothers bounce their babies – one, two, three – in the air and then, whoosh, plunge them into the water. The babies bob up like little surprised corks. None of them cries. We are supposed to swish the babies about on their backs, so I swish N a bit and he doesn't seem to mind too much. Then the teacher – who I am starting to dislike – tells us to swim on our fronts and let the babies hold on to our necks behind us. I don't think N knows how to hold onto my neck – he is only six months old; he has not learned how to hug me yet – but I am too scared to admit this to the teacher, who has already identified N and me as the problem couple. He tells me he will come over and help. I hoist N onto my shoulders in the way the teacher has shown us and wait while the others set off. The teacher arrives and puts a hand on N and tells me to swim, so I do a bit of slow breaststroke. N's arms are around my neck because the teacher is helping him hold on, but then I am aware of his slipping slowly off me and suddenly he is underwater. He comes up coughing and screaming and very red. I gather him up and hold him against me and he coughs and coughs and screams and coughs. The teacher looks sheepish and tells me N needs to get used to going underwater because it is the only way he will learn to hold on. I give him a stony look. N is still coughing like mad and the teacher tells me to hold him very upright as water may be stuck in his airways and he needs to get them clear. I hold the coughing N as upright as I can. He is making noisy retching sounds now and is still crying hard. The teacher smiles at him and says, 'Oh dear,' and I have to turn away from him because I am so angry. N is in such a panic that he seems to be finding it quite hard to breathe. The teacher suggests we go and sit on the steps at the side and we retreat gratefully. I try to distract N with floating plastic toys, but he is beside himself. He looks very small and very wet in his baby wetsuit and I feel like a very bad, very stupid mother for bringing him here.

After a few minutes cowering on the steps I decide we are going to get out; this has been quite enough. But the teacher spots me trying to escape and tells me it is better to stay in: if we leave, N will think he can always get himself out by crying. I want to laugh at him and tell him that N is only six months old, but I don't because I am a coward. For some reason I can't not do what this teacher tells me to do, so N and I sit it out on the steps while the other babies continue with the lesson. Finally it is time for the goodbye song and we are told we have to join in. We sing the song and get out, me feeling humiliated, N feeling cross and with water possibly still stuck somewhere in his throat because he is still spluttering slightly. And then it's back into the changing rooms where I boldly make a bid for a proper changing space so as not to have to change him on the sink. I get us showered and dressed as fast as I possibly can. One by one the other mothers come over to console me. They tell me how much their babies love these swimming classes and how N will learn to love them too. I am doubtful about this, but I try very hard to be nice and smile and look grateful for their wise words. I know they must think I have a difficult, screamy baby and I want to tell them that the opposite is true. I feel defensive of N. I manoeuvre us out of the changing rooms as quickly as I can manage. On the way out I have to buggy alongside a man who tells me that his baby (who has just come out of a swimming pool and isn't even wearing a coat!) used to hate swimming until he realised it was all his own fault. He tells me that as soon as he learned to relax in the water his baby started to enjoy it too. I feel like thumping him for his smugness, but I smile and nod and say I'm sure he is right, it must all be my fault and next time I will try harder to relax.

For various stupid reasons (because I have paid for the whole course upfront, because I convince myself N will like it next time), I take N back a week later. He hates the second class just as much as the first. This time, I summon up the courage to leave the pool early and ignore the teacher's disapproving looks. The nice thing about getting out early is not having to speak to all the other annoying mothers.

As we buggy off into the sunshine, I am overwhelmed by a sense of relief. We are never going back to those classes again. I am an adult and I no longer have to put up with aggressive PE-type teachers and nor does N. From now on, we will sit at home on Wednesdays and play with a rattle.

aving

At ten months, N starts to wave. The first person he waves at is my sister, as she is climbing into her car to drive off after lunch one day. She is waving bye-bye at him and he extends his arm to the side in return. I am not sure how deliberate the gesture is. But then a few days later my mother tells me he was trying to wave at a waitress in a restaurant. So I try waving at him to see what happens. I wave and wave and when I stop he extends his arm up and waggles his forearm up and down. It is oddly moving, because it seems to me that this wobbly waving is his first deliberate attempt to communicate with us. It is a caricature of a wave and it makes me laugh. He is very proud of himself for doing it. When I wave at him he has to stop and watch me. When I stop, he waves back. We are not allowed, it seems, to wave at each other at the same time. Later we meet up with another baby the same age, a girl, and she has just learned to wave too. I wave at her, and she responds with a neat, adult flick of the wrist and a professional wave of the hand, a bit like the Queen. Nothing like the full lower-arm flopping about that is N's version of the signal. I prefer N's way, though it looks like hard work.

eaning

In the beginning of the great food fight that is called weaning, I make the fruit and vegetable purées myself. I steam broccoli, pears (lots and lots of pears), apples, parsnips, carrots, cauliflower, plums, sweet potato. I put the steamed stuff into the hand blender and it comes out mushy. I pour the runny broccoli, the runny sweet potato, into lots of small, plastic cubes with lids. I pile these small plastic cubes into the freezer. The ice box is crammed full of little pots. When I need to feed N I take out one or two cubes and heat them in a saucepan. Then I try to spoon the anonymous warmed-up fruit or vegetable into his mouth. Most of it goes all over him, me and the floor. A tiny bit goes into his mouth.

I keep up the steaming and freezing for quite a while. But then I start to get bored of the same fruit and vegetables and I tell myself that if I am bored of them then N must be too, and indeed he doesn't seem very interested. So I buy colourful pouches full of baby food with 'organic' written all over them. They contain prunes and apricots and blueberries. N seems to like them. There is less angry pushing the spoon away. He starts to open his mouth wide for it. I go back to the supermarket and buy more packets and stuff the cupboard full of them. I put the steaming and freezing on indefinite hold.

N lives on these packets for a few months. And then, as with the formula when he was younger, I start to get the creeping feeling that I am a bad mother for feeding him from packets. One day, he refuses to touch the packets at all. He has just acquired two new teeth and he wants to use them on something other than mush. As N grizzles with hunger, I start to worry about what I can find to feed him. Do other mothers feel like this, or do they all know instinctively what their babies should be eating and when? N is watching me, expectant, as I shuffle about the kitchen. I take down the baby cookbook that a friend gave me, so far unopened. There is a section on chicken and I turn to it. There are chicken breasts in the fridge and I cut a chunk out of one of them and I heat a pan with butter and I cook it. I take out the packet of baby pasta bits that I bought many weeks ago in a sudden fit of confidence. The pasta shapes are tiny but I pour them into an adult-sized pan of boiling water. I decide to make a cheese sauce, but when I go back to the fridge I find we have no cheese. We don't have much of anything in our fridge – we never do – and I realise that now we are parents we can't responsibly lack cheese. Then I spot a lurking tub of Philadelphia and I take out a few spoonfuls and put it in a pan to melt. I decide broccoli florets, whole, not puréed, will be the perfect green accompaniment, so out comes the steamer. I'm getting into this. This is the baby equivalent of a three-course meal. I arrange the cut-up chicken breast, the mini pasta in cheese sauce and the broccoli florets on a plate. I pile the dirty pans and steamer equipment in the sink; the sink is full because I have used so many pans to make one tiny meal for one tiny person. I put the plate on the table and N in his high chair. I am nervous about his reaction. I know I will be upset if he doesn't like it.

I pile a bit of pasta onto a spoon. N opens his mouth wide. He chomps at the tiny shapes, sucks them onto his tongue. He chews, chews, chews and then swallows. He smiles. He licks his lips. He wants more. He has another spoonful and then another. He takes big bites from the strips of chicken. He likes the chicken especially. He bites the tops off the broccoli florets. Bits of broccoli scatter onto the floor, the chair, the table, his dungarees. N smiles and chews. He is a man enjoying a good meal.

This, the first proper dinner that I have made him, is a success. He loves my food. There will be no more packets (well, not so many). Between spoonfuls, I phone D at work to tell him the momentous news of N's first real meal. It is the evening of his press day at the paper. Things are usually rushed at this point: there is a deadline to meet; people want to go home. He takes the call on his mobile out on the office balcony. He wants to know every detail. 'He's eating the pasta? What, does he chew it? It doesn't get stuck?' I tell him this is indeed the case.

When N is finally full, I eat the last of his cheesy pasta. It isn't bad. I realise that in the years ahead I will be eating many meals like this – left-over children's food. It is a strange thought, a grown-up thought. With this first proper meal, it is as though I can suddenly start to contemplate N's childhood, the next stage beyond his babyhood.

hen will I sleep through the night?

N is one year old now and I still don't know the answer to this question. I am, however, starting to think that his not sleeping through might be my own fault. Because I don't trust him to sleep safely the whole night in his cot, he doesn't. I lie in bed while he sleeps in the next room, and I wait for him to wake up, and he does. It as though I have made it happen: I have willed him into waking up just by thinking about it. Babies go far away when they sleep, but they do not forget about you. They stay plugged in to your neuroses, into your fantasies. One night, I am asleep and N is asleep beside me. I dream I am being tickled. I wake up because of the tickling; it feels so real. Beside me, in his sleep, N suddenly giggles loudly. It is as if he has felt the same tickles, as if he has been having the same dream. Even asleep, he can read my mind.

ords

As he hits one year, N is starting to make words. He has been saying '*boooo*' for 'blue' in the *A E I O BLUE* picture for some time. But I'm now aware of him trying to make other words, too. I realise that whenever he picks up a book and dangles it in front of me to read to him, he is saying the same word, and the word is '*gook*'. I'm not sure how long he has been saying this – perhaps quite a while. I take the book that he is handing to me and say 'book' slowly and clearly a few times over. He picks up a different book and says '*gook*' again. He can say the letter 'b' but he does not think it applies to these things. We look at a book with a pig on its cardboard page. I say 'pig'. N watches my mouth as I say it. '*Pppp*,' he says slowly and carefully. '*Pppp*.' This is his first 'p' sound. He can't quite get to the whole pig yet, but he is trying to copy what I am saying. This seems to me very grown-up behaviour indeed.

ork

On my first day back at work, everyone asks if I have a photo of N. But I have deliberately not brought one with me. I know that if I have one in my office, I will keep looking at it, and that when I look at it I will want to be back home with him, not in a tower block several miles away.

After saying hello to my boss I go into my own office and sit behind my desk. There is evidence of someone else's sandwich crumbs on the surface, and various sticky patches, where someone has been (so I am told) doing a bit of spray-mounting in my absence. When I try and turn my computer on I can't log in as me, even though I've been doing this remotely from home for months. So I spend most of the morning on the phone to the IT helpdesk, trying to persuade them to fix it. This sort of thing is what happens on your first day at work. Because this, I slowly realise, is what it is: my first day back, but also, in a way, my first day ever. I am the new girl all over again. There are people in this office I have never met before and who have never met me. They probably wonder what exactly I do.

At some point in the afternoon I realise that my phone extension has changed. No one has told me it is different, but there is a new number on the handset, which rings when I get someone to dial it. Reception still have me listed under my old number. It takes a good while to convince them to change my number in their database. I spend the day doing mundane things like this. I send my first emails telling the people I need to tell that I am back. I also chat with various colleagues who want to know about N, or who say they do. I try to keep my descriptions of him short and to the point. 'He's very well,' I say, and then steer the conversation somewhere else. I will not let them define me in this way.

While I am in the office, N is at home with my parents, who have come down for the day to look after him. I call often to find out what is happening. The office has its own life, and I was part of this life before N was part of mine. Here, in this building, with its unchanging routines (its schedule of meetings; its official hours; its regular deadlines; its annual programmes), it is theoretically possible for me to forget about the fact of N's existence. Here I am in a parallel universe, and it has swallowed me up whole, just as it did before.

Even so, by mid-afternoon on this, my first day back, I am clock-watching. I need, want, have to get back to him. It is a shock to realise that, after nine months, and with a baby now, my time is no longer my own. At five I run down the stairs, for the bus, for the train, and arrive back home, breathless from running, wet from the after-office rain. N is sitting happily next to my mother on the sofa. He is fine, he is well. I am filled with relief to be back here with him, until I remember that I am going to have to leave him to go to work again.

orrying

There are some things I worry more about now that I have N. I worry more about getting ill and dying. I check myself for lumps and bumps, scrutinise moles. I have always been a hypochondriac, but it has got much worse since N was born. I have more to lose these days. And there's not just me to think about; N would lose his mother, too. I wish I could shake it, this nagging sense that something fatal might be just around the corner. But I know it might be. My friend J is seriously ill with cancer. Her baby, G, is six months older than N. When we meet up we try not to talk about it. We go to the park or the zoo and talk about our boys instead. But right now she is too ill to go out. A mother with a young baby can be given just months to live. This is not supposed to happen.

riting

I have been writing this in fits and starts, usually while N has been sleeping – during his daytime naps, or after he has gone to bed in the evening. I have wanted to try and record him as a baby because it all feels so fleeting and slippery, as though it could just slide away out of view for ever if I do not pin it to the page. Sometimes I have written bits while N plays on the floor next to me or reads one of his books. I will sit and type and look over at him and feel relieved that he is occupied doing whatever it is he is doing, and then I will suddenly be struck by how perverse the whole thing is, because here I am typing about N from this distance instead of being down there properly with him. Then I feel a rush of panic because I know I should be making the most of his every moment, because this stage will be so very brief – this, after all, is what I have just been writing about. So I close the laptop and sit down and read a book to him, and I play with the things in his treasure basket with him, and I only go back to the computer once he is asleep in his cot and there is nothing to miss. While I am typing I am, of course, not doing laundry and not making dinner and not making home-cooked non-jar food for N. I am thrilled not to be doing these things, but sometimes briefly guilty (especially about the food).

Writing this has been one way of bridging the gap between the old me and the new mother-of-N me. New mothers need ways of getting by and I suspect typing this has been part of mine (along with the obsessive diary-filling). I think part of sitting here and typing away like this is about saying, 'I am a mother, but I am still here; I haven't gone anywhere, not really. Look, here is the proof.' It is, I suspect, about writing myself back into the picture.

Xenophobia

N and I catch the bus north from our house. The route passes through Stamford Hill, where a lot of Hasidic Jews live. Various soberly dressed mothers and their children board the bus and it starts to get quite crowded. A very pale boy with a skull cap and round wire glasses and long red ringlets presses up against N's buggy and peers into it. N has been sitting quite peacefully until this point, but he looks back at the pale boy looking at him and he screams and screams. The screaming is very loud and goes on and on as the boy carries on peering in. I am horrified by N's screaming and can't think what to do. Finally, the boy pulls away from the buggy when the bus slows; he gets off and N stops screaming. He is calm again, looking around happily.

We get off the bus a few stops on and I think about the branch of the family N gets his red hair from: the 'Ginger Birnes'. They live on the other side of London and are Orthodox Jews, all with red hair. In some ways, red-headed N was screaming at a version of his own self.

-ray

When N is a few months old we have to take him back to the hospital for a hip scan – a modern alternative to an X-ray to check the joints. N was breech before he turned so the doctors warned us we would have to come in for this. Apparently, when a baby is breech sometimes their hips don't fuse properly. If there is a problem, N may need an operation. This is what the hip scan is supposed to find out.

D and I carry N into the darkened room. D unpoppers the legs of N's babygro and takes his nappy off, as instructed by the doctor. He lays N on his side on a small metal trolley. It looks rather like a metal butcher's block. I flutter, hopelessly, at the side of the room. N looks so helpless and small on the trolley, I can't stand it. But D is in charge. He tends him like a sympathetic nurse. He holds him down first on his right side, then on his left, as the doctor runs the wand over each hip in turn. Images of N's bones, his joints, flash up on the screen. I am reminded of our early scans of him, those first glimpses. The doctor moves her index finger along the images. She is explaining their shapes to us, but I can't concentrate. I only snap to attention at the end of her explanation when she tells us that N's hips are normal. There will be no further scans and no operation. We dress N again and thank the doctor. The three of us leave the room unburdened.

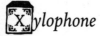ylophone

N has two of these, both made out of wood. At nine months he works out how to hold the beater and hit the notes with it. He hits them very hard.

oga

One of the things I do on maternity leave to get us both out of the house is mother and baby yoga. In these classes, we mothers do a bit of yoga for ourselves – which mainly involves stretching our legs a little and then lying out on the floor to recover, trying to relax while someone else's baby cries close by – and we also 'do yoga' on our babies. This involves dangling them upside down by their ankles and swinging them between our legs. Unsurprisingly, N loves it. He also loves looking at the teacher. He watches her for almost the whole hour and sneaks her little secret smiles. In return, the teacher sometimes lets N cuddle the teddy bear she uses to demonstrate her baby yoga moves. It dawns on me that N is trying to become the teacher's pet. I wonder if this is something he will keep up when he gets to school.

oghurt

Yoghurt is both extremely messy and one of N's favourite foods. I sometimes find it in my hair, smeared on the underside of the table, in blobs on the floor somewhere in the vicinity of the high chair. It gets everywhere.

You get used to it

'You get used to it,' is what mothers with older children would say to me about the experience of going back to work with a baby. And it is true, you do. After my early panics, as the weeks go by I find myself falling back into office life and its routines. I keep new hours – nine to five – and I generally leave on time. I start to realise it is important to have this other life – this working life – in which I am allowed to have an opinion about things, about whether they are good or bad or in need of improvement, and if they are in need of improvement in which particular ways. I even start to think, after a few months back at work, that I need the time away from N. I am surprised at myself for acknowledging it, and a little sad, too. There was a time when I dreaded the thought that I would one day leave him; now I feel that leaving him is something I have to do. I am not sure how this has happened and I worry something may have been broken along the way.

oo

N's grandmother buys him membership to the zoo as a first birthday present. D and I take him as soon as there is a non-rainy Sunday. He has been here before – we came with J and G when he was seven months old – and he liked it well enough then, but he is older now, and I am guessing that he will be enthralled by the animals, captivated by the strangeness of the monkeys, fascinated by the tallness of the giraffes. We push him round in his buggy past stripy zebras and sleeping lions. He hardly seems to notice them. Perhaps they are too far away and too camouflaged – they are behind glass or fenced off. N's non-reaction is obscurely disappointing. But then we stop in front of a cage of toucans. N looks up at them and stares. Then he laughs. A toucan flaps its wings and flies round the cage and lands and N laughs. He knows what it is going to do next. It flaps its wings and takes off and flies around and lands. He laughs again. We buggy him into the aquarium, a crumbling, 1920s bunker full of tanks of brightly coloured fish, and N squeals with excitement, just as he did when he came here almost half his life ago. We lift him out of his buggy and he tries to hit the fish as they swim past behind the glass, just as he did the first time. Since he is so grown-up now – he is a year old, for heaven's sake! – I had thought he would have moved on to other things. But it is the fish he loves the best. He is older, bolder, but still the same.

While I am walking round the zoo with N today as part of his birthday treat, I am thinking about J. When we came here with J and G, J was already seriously ill, but we still made a day of it because that was what she wanted. She was on her feet the whole time, pushing the buggy, carrying G. She wanted him to see everything; she had more energy than I did. Today, when N and I stand in front of the giraffe house, I remember J standing in just this spot holding G up to see the giraffes, and him studying their long necks. I want to cry as I stand here now. I am here, I know, to remember J, and our last proper day out together. J died eight days ago. She died the day after N's first birthday. When D and N and I sit outside the zoo café in the sunshine, I think that five months ago, J and G and N and I sat in this same spot. She should be sitting here as we are now, G chattering away beside her, in the way that N is chattering beside me. I know how lucky I am. None of this should be taken for granted.

Afterwords

N is one year old. Here are some of the things I have found myself unable to do so far:

- I have been unable to spend a night apart from N. I do not want to. Wherever I was, I would not be able to sleep.

- I have been unable to let N scream in his cot when he wakes in the night in the way the books say you should (they call this 'controlled crying'). This means that I often end up bringing N into bed with us in the middle of the night. I imagine this is a very bad habit I have got us into. But it means we all get some sleep.

- I have been unable to put N's tiny baby clothes away in the loft. I don't like thinking he has no more use for them.

- I have been unable to make much time to see friends who do not have babies – I do not seem to have room for a social life.

◆ I have been unable to get N christened at the church over the road, which means we will now need to move house when it's time for him to go to school since they will know for sure that we are heathens.

And here are some of the things I have been able to do:

◆ I have managed to raise a healthy one-year-old. A one-year-old!

◆ I have managed to go back to work and do my job.

◆ I have managed to find someone to look after N while I am at work and just about afford to pay for it.

◆ I have managed to get down to a size fourteen.

◆ I have managed, on the whole, to stay sane.

◆ I have managed to read books and occasionally go to the cinema or for an evening meal. (A proper social life I can do without. The odd trip to the cinema I cannot.)

◆ I have managed to enjoy having N more than anything else in the world.

This second list strikes me as not bad going. I am not going to worry too much about the first one.

Acknowledgements

Thanks to Tracy Bohan at The Wylie Agency. Thanks also to Sarah Caro, Rukhsana Yasmin, Anna-Marie Fitzgerald, Daniel Crewe and Diana Broccardo at Profile. Thanks to Sarah Lee, Anna Brocklehurst, Max Brocklehurst, Micaela Soar, Laura Soar, Deborah Jones and Hannah Bagshaw. I'm grateful to have known the friendship and support of Joanna Gallagher, first in the writing and then in the baby business.

Thanks to my parents.

Thank you, of course, to D and N.